RAISING A GODLY FAMILY

In An Ungodly World

By

Raul Ries

SLYP
somebody
loves you
publishing
Diamond Bar, California

Raising a Godly Family in an Ungodly World
Copyright © 2008 by Somebody Loves You Media Group
First printing © 1998
Revised edition © 2008
2nd printing, 2010

Published by Somebody Loves You Publishing
22324 Golden Springs Drive
Diamond Bar, Ca 91765-2449

Library of Congress Control Number: 2007907657

This book was edited from a series of Bible studies on marriage and family by Raul Ries and published by Somebody Loves You Publishing.

All Scripture quotations in this book are taken from the *Holy Bible,* New King James Version, copyright © 1979, 1980, 1982 by Thomas Nelson, Inc. Used by permission.

Due to the holy nature of God, the first letter of all references to Him, His holy name and His Word have been capitalized.

Words or phrases in brackets are not part of the original text. They have been added for clarification.

For further information and resources contact:
Somebody Loves You Media Group
22324 Golden Springs Drive
Diamond Bar, CA 91765-2449
(800) 634-9165
slymediagroup@somebodylovesyou.com
www.somebodylovesyou.com

ISBN: 978-1-934820-01-8

Printed in the United States of America

Somebody Loves You Media Group

Books by Raul Ries:

Doctrines: A Simplified Road Map of Biblical Truth

From Fury to Freedom

Raising A Godly Family In An Ungodly World

Hear What the Spirit Is Saying

Seven Steps to a Successful Marriage

God Answers Prayer

Five Deadly Vices

Understanding God's Compassion

Wake Up! Time Is Short

Follow Me

Practical Living from God's Word

Somebody Loves You Growth Book

Things of the Spiritual Realm:
Angels, Physical Attacks, Satan and Warfare

Living Above Your Circumstances–
A Study in the Book of Daniel

Books By Sharon Ries:

My Husband, My Maker

The Well-Trodden Path
(booklet)

Books by Various Authors:

Patriarcas en la Carcel
by Ruth Smith

The Philosophy of Ministry of Calvary Chapel
by Chuck Smith

Films in DVD* by Raul Ries:

Fury to Freedom

Taking the Hill:
A Warrior's Journey Home

A Quiet Hope:
A Film for Vietnam Veterans

A Venture in Faith:
The History and Philosophy of the Calvary Chapel Movement

*All DVD's are in English and Spanish

S.L.Y. Media Group
22324 Golden Springs Drive
Diamond Bar, CA 91765-2449

slymediagroup@somebodylovesyou.com
www.somebodylovesyou.com
(800) 634-9165

Table of Contents

A Note from Pastor Raul

PART ONE – Become a Godly Spouse

Chapter 1 – Becoming a Godly Parent
Begins with Becoming a Godly Spouse...................... 11

Chapter 2 – The Role of the Husband......................... 15

Chapter 3 – The Role of the Wife............................. 19

PART TWO – Become a Godly Parent

Chapter 4 – The Role of a Godly Parent 25

Chapter 5 – Be a Living Example of Christ 29

Chapter 6 – Be a Leader in the Home
Establish Parental Authority............................. 33

Chapter 7 – Teach Your Children about God 37

Chapter 8 – Train Your Children in the Way
They Should Go 45

Chapter 9 – Discipline Your Children In the Lord............. 57

Chapter 10 – Provide for Your Children's Well-Being 63

A Final Note 67

Scriptures to Help the Family............................... 68

A Note from Pastor Raul ...

According to the Bible, the family was the first social structure God created. Unfortunately, as we look around our world today, we see that the family unit is deteriorating. Quite literally, the family is dying. With this death, we are witnessing the rise of crime, juvenile delinquency, drugs, sexual immorality and gang affiliations, along with widespread hatred and rebellion.

Our nation's youth are in trouble and High School campuses are becoming war zones — where, daily, teachers and students are in danger of school violence. All the while, our youth are not being educated. According to Richard Riley, former Secretary of Education, in 2006, more than 8 million U.S. students in grades 4-12 struggle to read, write and comprehend adequately.

Crime is up 500% since 1963 — the infamous year the Supreme Court decided prayer and the Bible did not belong in our nation's schools. Lawlessness in our streets is becoming the norm, with gang violence, rapes and drive-by shootings increasing. Promiscuity among the youth is on the rise with an estimated 180,000 young people infected every day in America with a Sexually Transmitted Disease (STD).

What is the answer?

There is only one thing that will turn us around — that is for God's people to get their lives right with the Lord and lay the foundation necessary to raise godly kids, which starts with godly parents.

Maybe you are engaged, a newlywed or have been married for years and already have a family. Regardless of your situation, my question to you is, "Where are you in your walk with Jesus Christ?"

Billy Graham says, "Apart from religious influence, the family is the most important unit of society. It would be well if every home were Christian. But we know that is not possible. The home can never exert their proper influence while ignoring the Biblical standards that God has set up. The Bible calls for discipline and a recognition of authority in the home. If children do not learn this at home, they will go out into society without the proper attitude towards authority and the law. There is always the exceptional child, but the average tells us that the child is largely what the home has made him or her. The only way to provide the right home for your children is to put the Lord above them and fully instruct them in the ways of the Lord. You are responsible, as parents, before God and before man, for your home — to provide for your children's needs."

Raising a Godly Family in an Ungodly World begins with you! Are you following Christ and being obedient to His Word? It is my prayer that as you read the following pages, you will be encouraged through God's Word to become a godly example to your children, and train up your children in the way they should go. May the Lord guide you and bless you as you bring your home under His authority…

Souls for Christ,

Raul

PART ONE

Become a Godly Spouse

···1···

Becoming a Godly Parent Begins with Becoming a Godly Spouse

Does God have a purpose for your life? Your spouse? Your family? The answer is a resounding yes!

God ordained marriage as the foundation for the family unit. However, in our world today, we see the fundamental family unit being scorned and ripped apart. In its place, we see children brought up in homes where there is an absence of the father.

We also see a push for homosexuals to adopt and raise children as an alternate type of "family" unit; however, this is an abomination in God's eyes.

God's plan for the family unit is found in Genesis 2:18, *"And the Lord God said, 'It is not good that man should be alone; I will make him a helper comparable to him.'"*

A godly marriage is the foundation for a godly family. God saw that it was not good for man to be alone. He made the woman from man, and made her comparable to him. Together, as husband and wife, the two individuals become one. They are compatible with one another — loving each other, talking with one another, sharing life together, worshipping together and living as one.

Does this describe your marriage?

You may be reading this right now and saying, "Raul, you do not know my husband; you do not know my wife; we are totally opposite. Nothing seems compatible in our relationship."

God is not talking about your personalities. He is talking about your roles as husband and wife — and your relationship with Jesus Christ.

Billy Graham says, "The perfect marriage is a uniting of three persons — a man, a woman and God! That is what makes marriage holy. Faith in Christ is the most important of all principles in the building of a happy marriage and a happy home."

Do confusion, strife and tension dominate your marriage? Then it is a marriage devoid of God. Jesus Christ needs to be at the center of your marriage, and in order for Him to be at the center of your marriage, He needs to be at the center of your life!

I have counseled many couples in the course of ministry. Time and again, I have found that the underlying issue in every marital problem is the spouse's relationship with the Lord. When God created Adam, he was in constant communion with Him. The Lord saw Adam's need for a helpmate — a companion — and created Eve from Adam's rib (God created woman from the closest part to man's heart). Together, they dwelt in the Garden of Eden, having constant communion with God. This was God's perfect design for marriage — God, man and woman, but then sin entered the world. Satan deceived Eve, Adam abdicated his role of leadership and both husband and wife were separated from God.

We live in a fallen world and are a sinful people, but Christ died for our sins and has reconciled us back to God. Now, in Him, we can live the life that God designed for us — a life of constant communion with Him. When we, as individuals, turn to the Lord, we become one with Him and with each other. This is the key to our married life.

Marriage is not always easy. There are going to be problems in married life. However, as husbands and wives come together in the Lord, they grow in God's purpose for them.

Though men and women are comparable to each other in God's eyes, He has designed specific roles for each one in order to create unity and harmony in the home. This provides a nurturing environment for children to be raised in the ways of the Lord.

· · · 2 · · ·
The Role of the Husband

In Genesis 2:24 the Lord commands, *"Therefore a man shall leave his father and mother and be joined to his wife, and they shall become one flesh."*

God places the responsibility of marriage upon the man's shoulders. It is the husband's role to be responsible for his wife and home, for the Lord has put the husband in the role of leadership. In Ephesians 5:23, the Apostle Paul tells us, *"For the husband is the head of the wife, as also Christ is head of the church; and He is the Savior of the body."*

In homes today, there is a lack of leadership by the husband. Many women feel burdened with the role of headship, or have taken it on themselves, because the men have abdicated their role before Christ.

As a godly husband, leadership is not a choice but a command of God. What does this leadership role entail?

Leadership includes:
• **Loving your wife** — serving her as Christ served the church. This means looking after your wife's needs and dying to self.

- **Commitment** — living with your wife for life.

- **Being high priest of the home** — the husband is to love his wife by being the spiritual leader of the home. You are called to lead your wife in prayer, read the Word with her, have family devotions and instigate involvement in your local church. Ephesians 5:25-27 says, *"Husbands, love your wives, just as Christ also loved the church and gave Himself for her, that He might sanctify and cleanse her with the washing of water by the Word, that He might present her to Himself a glorious church, not having spot or wrinkle or any such thing, but that she should be holy and without blemish."*

- **Honoring your wife** — the Lord is calling you to be understanding and compassionate towards your wife, treating her with gentleness and honor. I Peter 3:7 states, *"Husbands, likewise, dwell with them with understanding, giving honor to the wife, as to the weaker vessel, and as being heirs together of the grace of life, that your prayers may not be hindered."*

- **Provision** — you are to provide the basic physical needs for your wife and home.

At this point, husbands reading this book might be shaking their heads saying, "Raul, how do I do this? I have fallen miserably short of being a godly leader in my home." Let me remind you that you cannot be a godly husband in your own strength and abilities. You need to be in close communion with the Lord, and you need to be filled with His Holy Spirit in order to fulfill your God-given role. But let me assure you — it can be done! The Lord does not give us a command that He does not give us the strength and ability to fulfill! If you have abdicated the role of leadership in your home, repent and turn to God. A right relationship with the Lord will enable you to see your wife as a gift from God, and a right relationship with the Lord will enable you to treat your wife as God intended. The Lord wants you to fulfill your role. He is waiting to bless your marriage and your home. It is God's purpose that your home will glorify Him!

Let me leave you with this quote from Henry Varley. He writes, "The world has yet to see what God can do with, and for, and through a man who is fully and wholly consecrated to Him."

・・・ 3 ・・・
The Role of the Wife

Unfortunately, women have undergone tremendous pressure and confusion regarding their role in marriage. However, the Bible is very clear. Just as the husband is called to a role of godly leadership, the wife is called to a role of submission, in the Lord. The Word of God sets forth the order of submission. First, it declares in Ephesians 5:21, that we are all to submit one to another in the fear of God. Ephesians 5:22 then adds, *"Wives, submit to your own husbands, as to the Lord."* What does the role of submission entail?

- **Respecting your husband** — respect the position of godly leadership that God has given him. Show honor and consideration to your husband's God-given responsibilities and build him up in the Lord. Ephesians 5:33 says, *". . . let the wife see that she respects her husband."*

- **Loving your husband** — overlook offenses with a forgiving heart. Look for the best about your husband, not the worst, and look out for his greatest interest.

- **Obeying your husband in the Lord** — this means that you are to give your husband input and wisdom. When the final decision is made, you must be obedient to the godly authority of your husband — whether you agree with him or not.

At this point, if you are a woman, you may be saying, "Raul, my husband is not a spiritual leader. Why should I submit to him?" Let's face it, ladies, men can be creeps! However, you are to be obedient to God's Word as a Christian woman. God does not ask you to fulfill your role only if your husband is fulfilling his. Rather, God is asking you to be obedient to him, in the Lord. However, God never declared that you are to submit or obey unrighteous, ungodly authority that will lead you, or your family, to sin, resulting in a life of disobedience to God. Acts 5:29 says, ". . . *'We ought to obey God rather than men.'"*

Remember, God honors a wife's obedience. I Peter 3:1-6 states, *"Wives, likewise, be submissive to your own husbands, that even if some do not obey the Word, they, without a word, may be won by the conduct of their wives, when they observe your chaste conduct accompanied by fear. Do not let your adornment be merely outward — arranging the hair, wearing gold, or putting on fine apparel — rather let it be the hidden person of the heart, with the incorruptible beauty of a gentle and quiet spirit, which is very precious in the sight of God. For in this manner, in former times, the holy women who trusted in God also adorned themselves, being submissive to their own husbands, as Sarah obeyed Abraham, calling him Lord, whose daughters you are if you do good and are not afraid with any terror."*

Today, it seems like people do not want to work on their marriages but that is what it takes — work. Men must learn to be spiritual leaders. Women must learn to submit themselves to their husbands, in the Lord.

What foundation are you laying in your home? Are you building up your marriage or tearing it down? Remember, godly families begin with godly marriages. Take the first step now — repent and become the spouse that God wants you to be.

PART TWO

Become a Godly Parent

· · · 4 · · ·

The Role of a Godly Parent

God is not neutral. In Joshua 24:15 we are told, *"...choose for yourselves this day whom you will serve...."*

The beginning of wisdom is establishing Jesus Christ as the Lord of your home.

In Chapter 24 of the book of Joshua, we find that Joshua is now old and ready to die. His days on earth are winding down, so he gathers all of the people of his family together and exhorts them to serve the Lord. Many in the world were following false gods. Many of God's people had turned their backs on the ways of the Lord and had gone back to a carnal life. It is in this setting that Joshua boldly declares, *"...But as for me and my house, we will serve the Lord"* (Joshua 24:15).

As a pastor, I see this even today. Many parents have turned their backs on the Lord and are serving their own interests and selfish desires. Because of this, they do not want to take responsibility for their own children. Instead, many parents would love to blame the church, the nursery, Sunday school or public education for the way their kids have turned out as adults. However, the Bible never instructed the church or government to raise, protect or train children. No, God has specifically given "parents" the responsibility to nurture, guide, teach, train and discipline their children. The Lord has also given guidelines and insight as to how children are to be raised.

I like this quote from V. Raymond Edman, "I am persuaded that if mothers and fathers would earnestly seek to know the meaning of full consecration in God's service, they would have clear guidance in the rearing of their children."

As a parent, you need to determine that your "house" will serve the Lord.

We live in an ungodly world. The values that rule our society are not the same values that rule God's people. At one time, the gap between the two was not so wide. There was an era, especially in America, when the values that ruled God's people were the same values that ruled our schools and justice system. However, that has changed. We are witnessing, in our world, what took place in the days of the book of Judges (in the Old Testament). *"In those days there was no king in Israel; everyone did what was right in his own eyes"* (Judges 17:6).

That is the philosophy of today, "I'm going to do my own thing."

It seems that this philosophy has really affected the home. It has affected husbands, wives, single parents and those that are not married. Worst of all, it has spiraled down to affect the children of this generation. In Judges 2:10 we read, *"When all that generation had been gathered to their fathers, another generation arose after them who did not know the Lord nor the work which He had done for Israel."*

The parents in the second generation did not acknowledge the Lord as the ruler of their lives. Instead, they did what was right in their own eyes — they did their own thing. Turning their backs on God's Lordship in their lives resulted in children who knew nothing of God or His work. These children ended up doing evil in His sight, as well.

I believe we have the same problem today. Parents may declare they are Christians, but they do not submit to the Lordship of Jesus Christ, so their homes are filled with confusion and disorder.

God's design for your home is one of order. As a parent, you are responsible for your children because they were given to you by God to be brought up in the ways of the Lord.

Only when you make Jesus Christ Lord of your lives and your home, will you be a godly parent, raising godly children.

God gives parents a promise. *"Train up a child in the way he should go, and when he is old he will not depart from it"* (Proverbs 22:6).

Let's take a closer look at the responsibilities of being a godly parent.

· · · 5 · · ·

Be a Living Example of Christ

"Do as I say, not as I do."

How many times have we heard that, growing up? Maybe, you never heard that as a child — but chances are you did. Perhaps, you have found yourself echoing those same words. The Bible teaches that we are to be examples, in everything we do. As Christians, we are to emulate Christ in our lives, so as to bring the ungodly to repentance. In our employment, we should be an example of diligence, perseverance, hard work and the list goes on.

Yet, many times, as parents, we fail to recognize the obvious. We need to practice what we preach and be an example to our children.

Children mimic what they hear and see. How many times does a child repeat a phrase that they have heard from their parents? Many times, our children take on mannerisms and bad habits that we ourselves display to them.

How can you tell your child not to lie, when you lie? How can you tell your child not to take drugs, when you take drugs? How can you tell your child not to drink, when you drink? The list is endless and I am sure you get my point.

When we do not live by example, we bring great inconsistency into our homes. As a parent, your actions must back up your words. Not only will your children take on your bad attitudes, actions and habits, but they will have a poor example of Christianity. Do you realize that when you live contrary to Christ's teachings, you are misrepresenting God before your children? How can you teach your children in God's ways, and then live contrary to them?

Stephen Green writes, "Only as genuine Christian holiness and Christlike love are expressed in the life of a parent, can the child have the opportunity to inherit the flame and not the ashes."

As parents, you are representatives of God. You have a great responsibility, before God and your children, to be obedient to the Word of the Lord. Yes, as parents, we need to be living examples of Christ. Now, that is not always easy because parents are not super humans, and we struggle daily with our flesh, sin and the devil. That is why it is so important to walk closely with the Lord by being in His Word on a daily basis.

Parents are not perfect. When you do make a mistake, when you misrepresent God, when you are a bad example, confess it to the Lord and to your children. Let your children see a right example of confession of sin and repentance. This can help them understand God's grace in their own lives and go far to nurture an atmosphere of respect.

What kind of example are you to your children? Does your walk match your talk? Keep in mind, as we go through the remaining responsibilities of parenthood, that you need to be a godly example in each aspect of parenting duties.

· · · 6 · · ·

Be a Leader in the Home
Establish Parental Authority

During the 1960's, there was a phrase used by the counter-revolution (the teenagers and young adults of the world) that simply stated, "Question authority." Unfortunately, that attitude has penetrated throughout recent generations. Those who were part of that counter culture are now parents — and many have not established any semblance of authority in the home.

Dr. Billy Graham writes, "Parents do wrong by failing to exercise wise and loving authority over their children. Children are born with an intimate instability and with a desire to be directed and guided by their parents. If they discover that their parents are weak instead of strong and incapable of leading them properly, their personality is affected, and they will then seek to find unwholesome and improper leadership with gangs and terror clubs and sadistic rings of other young people."

Godly parents need to establish strong parental authority in the home, based on the principles set forth in the Word of God.

One of the sad things, we see taking place today, is either the absence of the father in the home, or the father's lack of leadership. It seems to me, in our world today, we are in deep trouble when it comes to the role of the father. In many cases, fathers are abandoning their homes by excusing themselves from the leadership role God has called them to.

It has been reported, by a number of crime prevention agencies, that there is a far greater risk of young men joining gangs or getting involved in violent crime, when there is an absence of the father in the home. According to the Journal of Research of Crime and Delinquency, the best indicator of violent crimes in a community is not based on income and unemployment, but on the number of fatherless families.

The Family Research Council cites some tragic statistics in their crime surveys. They found that 60% of rapists came from single parent households, 72% of adolescent murders were from single parent homes and 70% of juveniles living in long-term correctional facilities were by-products of single parent homes.

Today, more than 18 million children are growing up in households without fathers.

Now, I am not putting down mothers or single parents. It is a very difficult job to raise children on your own — and many are doing a commendable job. However, it is important to recognize God's order for the family, and that order calls for both a father and mother to raise their children and establish their God-given authority in their home. Because God gave the man the role of spiritual headship in the marriage, he has also given the father the greater responsibility of establishing spiritual authority and leadership in the home. I Timothy 3:4 says, *". . . one who rules his own house well, having his children in submission with all reverence. . . ."*

Having worked in ministry for more than 36 years, my wife and I have counseled hundreds of women who have expressed their frustrations over their husband's lack of leadership in the home. For men reading this book, it may seem that I am beating this point to death, but I will say it again, YOU MUST TAKE THE SPIRITUAL LEADERSHIP ROLE IN YOUR HOME. If you have not done this, you need to repent now and do it!

Children need to see consistency and leadership in the home. They need to see a strong father and a strong mother, as well as unity between their parents. Children do not need to see their parents divided, going opposite ways and disagreeing. This only brings chaos into the home, with disunity creating confusion, and the child often playing the mother and the father against each other. They must know *". . . that the head of every man is Christ, the head of woman is man, and the head of Christ is God"* (1 Corinthians 11:3).

Parents, take control of your home. If you abdicate your authority, you will find that instead of God ruling your home, it will be Satan. He is the author of confusion, strife and every wicked thing. Being a godly parent means you are a person of authority to your children and a leader of the home. This is so important!

Ben Haden concludes, "A permissive home is a home where you don't love enough to exercise the authority God gave you."

· · · 7 · · ·

Teach Your Children About God

"Behold, children are a heritage from the Lord…" (Psalm 127:3).

The number one desire parents should have regarding their children is that they know God. The Lord has given children to you not only as a gift, but also as an investment, so you may teach them about God's love and His ways. He has not given you children so you can see a copy of yourself running around, nor has He given you children to abuse, ignore or mistreat. No, God has given you children so you may teach them about Him — so they would be drawn unto Him. Your children are on loan to you. It is an awesome responsibility, but the Lord gives us instruction as to what we are to do. By being obedient to His Word, God will give us the wisdom and the strength to teach our children about the ways of the Lord.

Whether your children are young or old, you know they are being influenced by the evilness of society. They are continually exposed to the evil of the world — whether it is television, movies, school or just running around with their friends — and your children are constantly being exposed to the world's values, thoughts, desires and temptations.

As parents, you are the source of God's light in your children's world. When they are young, you can shelter your children from many of the world's influences (such as television shows, certain movies, etc.), but as they get older, it becomes increasingly hard to filter out the evil influences upon them. That is why, as a parent, it is your job to present God's ideas, thoughts, values and desires to your children. I have broken down this role into three specific areas: The Word of God, Worship and Prayer.

The Word of God

God has placed the role of leader on the husband, and has placed the role of "High Priest," in the home, on the father as well. Though both parents are to teach their children the ways of God, it is up to the father to take the spiritual leadership in the home.

Moses tells us in Deuteronomy 6:6-7, *"And these words which I command you today shall be in your heart. You shall teach them diligently to your children, and shall talk of them when you sit in your house, when you walk by the way, when you lie down, and when you rise up."*

As a father, you need to take the leadership role in teaching your family God's Word. Now, I am not saying that you need to give them a three-hour Bible study every night! If you do that, your children will become frustrated and turned off to the Gospel of Jesus Christ. It is wise, however, to establish a family devotional time every day.

You are responsible, before the Lord, to teach the Word of God to your family. It is through God's Word that we learn about the Lord's love for us, our own sinfulness, our need for Jesus Christ and the way of salvation. The Word of God is also the fundamental tool in teaching your children about right and wrong — filling their minds with God's truth and teaching them in the ways of righteousness.

It is the role of both parents to be continually sharing the Word of God with their children. Yet today, we do not see the Word taught in the home. In fact, we see parents being disobedient to the Word of God and compromising their own faith. Sometimes it is a problem of busyness. However, if you are too busy to be in the Word yourself, what are you teaching your children?

Jesus tells us, *"But seek first the kingdom of God and His righteousness, and all these things shall be added to you"* (Matthew 6:33).

If you are too busy to be in God's Word, you are TOO busy! Remember to put your priorities in order. The problem in many homes, today, is that the Word of God is not being proclaimed and applied! You wonder why your children do not want to behave and why your house is out of order. Get into God's Word as a family.

You need to spend time sitting with your children and teaching them God's Word. Make time in your busy schedule to regularly share the Scriptures with them — teach them of God's love, care and greatness. Find a time that is best for everyone; maybe in the morning or after dinner. It does not need to be a long process, but it needs to be consistent and on a daily basis.

One way to share the Word is to read a Bible story to your children every night before bed. There are enough examples in God's Word that share about what He has done for His people to last your child's lifetime. Remember, the Bible is the Word of God — teach all of it to your kids.

You do not have to be a theologian or a pastor to teach your children the Word. There are many good devotional books that you can read together as a family, as well.

Moses, in referring to the Word of God, tells us in Deuteronomy 6:8-9, *"You shall bind them* [God's Word] *as a sign on your hand, and they shall be as frontlets between your eyes. You shall write them on the doorposts of your house and on your gates."*

Practically speaking, God wants you to put His Word in places where the entire household can see it. Some people hang pictures with Scriptures on them around the house, while others display Scripture verses in the bathroom, kitchen, garage and play room.

One great place to put framed Scripture verses is in your children's bedrooms. When our kids were growing up, Sharon and I put the Ten Commandments in each of our boys' rooms. That way, when they lay down to sleep, they saw the Ten Commandments and when they awoke for the day, they saw the Ten Commandments. The more your kids see Scriptures, the more God's Word sticks in their minds. Be creative. Be consistent. In one form or another, make sure you teach the Word of God to your children on a daily basis.

The Psalmist wrote in Psalm 119:9, *"How can a young man cleanse his way? By taking heed according to Your Word."* God's Word cleanses. Your entire family is exposed, daily, to the world's value system. Your children, as well as yourselves, need to be cleansed in the Word of God on a daily basis. Fathers, take the lead in sharing the Word of God with your family. God's Word never comes back void. Instilling the Scriptures into your children at an early age will help them to walk with God in their adult life.

Worship

In Job 1:5 we read, *"So it was, when the days of feasting had run their course, that Job would send and sanctify them* [his children], *and he would rise early in the morning and offer burnt offerings according to the number of them all. For Job said, 'It may be that my sons have sinned and cursed God in their hearts.' Thus Job did regularly."*

Notice, Job took upon himself the role of priest in the home. He made intercession on behalf of his family and offered sacrifices for their sins. He consecrated his life and that of his family's to the

Lord. Job had his priorities right. He knew God, and put God first in his own life, as well as making sure that God was first in his family's lives.

Job's children saw their father's concern for their consecration to God. They saw that Job was concerned with the problems and sins they had, and he would present them before the Lord. Job served his children as a living example of worship. He taught them how to worship God through his actions.

How about you? Are you teaching your children to worship God through your actions, or are you teaching them not to worship God?

In Proverbs 1:7, we can see King Solomon imparting wisdom to his children by saying, *"The fear of the Lord is the beginning of knowledge, but fools despise wisdom and instruction."*

Notice the godly counsel Solomon gave to his children. He taught them what worshipping God was all about. He told them that the fear of the Lord was the beginning of knowledge. What does he mean by *fear?* The Hebrew word for *fear* in this passage refers to reverence. Webster's Dictionary defines *reverence* as a feeling of deep respect, love and awe! That is the essence of worship! God is holy, and those who worship Him must worship Him in spirit and truth. If we do not reverence God, we become fools. We become stupid because we follow our own sinful ways and the ways of the world rather than the ways of God.

Fathers, Mothers too, you need to teach your children how to worship God by example.

Prayer

"The family that prays together stays together." You may be tired of hearing that slogan, but it is true. Prayer is the glue that binds families together. In many ways, prayer is a form of worship — but it is also the key element in family fellowship.

Maybe, right now, your home is a disaster with yelling, screaming, fighting and turmoil like you cannot believe. Let me ask you, when the kids started to get on your nerves today, did you scream or did you pray? It is our natural, sinful flesh that reacts first and then prays, but God wants our spirit in control, not our flesh.

As parents, you need to stop yelling and screaming and start praying. Fathers, first thing in the morning, lead your family in prayer. Mothers, take a moment and pray with your children during the day.

I have seen the difference prayer can make, in my own home. Prayer brings peace. It aligns us with God's will and helps us to turn our eyes on Jesus, rather than on the situation or crises at hand. Your children need to see praying parents. Pray as a family for needs, direction, guidance and strength. Teach your children to turn to

God in prayer when a difficult situation arises or when they need wisdom. Allow your children to see you when you are broken by God, humbled and on your knees, praying in tears.

If you do family devotions in the evening, make sure you allow time for your children to also pray. Prayer is our means of communication with the Lord — and yet, it is often the last thing we do.

Parents, take the time to pray for and with your children. You will see the difference it makes in your home.

· · · *8* · · ·

Train Your Children in the Way They Should Go

Proverbs 22:6 tells us, *"Train up a child in the way he should go, and when he is old he will not depart from it."*

I found the dictionary definition of the word *train* interesting. Webster's Dictionary says "to train" means "to guide the mental, moral, etc. development of" or "to instruct so as to make proficient." In Hebrew, it means, "to initiate, discipline, dedicate or consecrate."

God wants parents to train their children. We are to teach them about God and His ways, as well as, teach them how to live their lives in a way that glorifies God. Proverbs 22:6 gives a promise to parents. If you take responsibility for your children and, when they are babies, begin to teach them God's Word, how to live a righteous life by loving God and loving others as themselves, that child will not depart from God's ways. That is a promise. God's Word does not come back void.

Your children do have a will of their own and you cannot force God down their throats, but if you are diligent to raise your children in God's ways, and are an example in your home, they will remember the teaching and return to it later in life.

I have listed three specific areas where we should train our children in God's ways. These include fleeing sin and resisting evil, responsibility and respect.

Fleeing Sin and Resisting Evil

In the book of Proverbs, Solomon gave wisdom to his children. He instructed them and trained them up in the ways of the Lord. One particular point that Solomon drove home to his kids was the matter of fleeing from sin. Read what Solomon said to his children:

"My son, if sinners entice you, do not consent. If they say, 'Come with us, let us lie in wait to shed blood; let us lurk secretly for the innocent without cause; let us swallow them alive like Sheol, and whole, like those who go down to the Pit; we shall find all kinds of precious possessions, we shall fill our houses with spoil; cast in your lot among us, let us all have one purse.' My son, do not walk in the way with them, keep your foot from their path" (Proverbs 1:10-15).

It is clear in this passage that Solomon trained his child to flee from those who would entice him to sin. Today, I hear so many stories of parents who are upset because their children have joined a gang, and they do not know what to do. The problem is that they never trained their children to flee from these types of people or activities. Solomon told his son, in this passage, to stay away from gangs — from people who want to kill other people and steal. Though it was back in biblical times, you can easily read this portion of Scripture and picture gangs and drive-by shootings.

Parents, you need to train your children to flee from those things that are sinful and harmful to them. You need to do this by instructing them in the Word of God. Solomon tells parents how to deal with their children, as in the above passage, so they do not get involved in gangs, alcohol, sexual immorality, etc.

In Proverbs 20:1, the Bible says, *"Wine is a mocker, strong drink is a brawler, and whoever is led astray by it is not wise."* This Scripture tells kids why they are not to drink — what alcohol will do to them and how it will make them stupid.

In I Corinthians 6:18, we are instructed, *"Flee sexual immorality. Every sin that a man does is outside the body, but he who commits sexual immorality sins against his own body."* This Scripture tells your children to flee from sexual sin and why.

Throughout the Bible, there is instruction to flee from sin, and when you train your children, you give them the Word of God. Do not give them your philosophy — lecturing them. They do not want to hear what you have to say — they want to know what God has to say. Remember, God's Word does not come back void. Your words will come back void, but not God's. The Word of God takes hold of your children's hearts and minds. The Holy Spirit reminds them of what they have learned and brings conviction. The Word of God leads and guides children to knowledge and wisdom, teaching them how to act as young men or young women.

As parents, our job is to train our children, through the Word of God, how to flee from sin. Now, you may be saying, "Raul, we have been doing that. We have been sharing the Word of God with our kids and we have been doing these things you are saying, but one of our kids is rebelling and running with the wrong crowd. What did we do wrong?"

Going back to Proverbs 1, in verses 20-22, it says, *"Wisdom* [God's Word] *calls aloud outside; she raises her voice in the open squares. She cries out in the chief concourses, at the openings of the gates in the city she speaks her words: 'How long, you simple ones, will you love simplicity? For scorners delight in their scorning, and fools hate knowledge.'"*

Notice what it says. The problem is, they hate what God has to say and that is going to happen sometimes. Remember, your children are sinners too, and they have a choice whether to follow God or not. Your job, as parents, is to instruct them and train them in the ways of the Lord from the time they are babies. Be an example to them in the home and do what you are supposed to do. There may be a time of rebellion, and your children may have to learn the hard way.

In fact, as we continue in Proverbs 1, we read in verses 23-26, *"Turn at My rebuke; surely I will pour out My Spirit on you; I will make My words known to you. Because I have called and you refused, I have stretched out My hand and no one regarded, because you disdained all My counsel, and would have none of My rebuke, I also will laugh at your calamity; I will mock when your terror comes."*

God is saying; if you do not want to turn from these sins, you are going to learn the hard way. As parents, we need to realize that our children, especially when they hit the teen years and then adulthood, have a choice to follow God or rebel. God is saying; if they choose to rebel, then they are going to learn the hard way. Remember the prodigal son. He chose to rebel, at one point, but, eventually, he learned his lesson, repented and returned home.

There is always a promise with God. In concluding Proverbs 1, we read verse 33, *"But whoever listens to Me will dwell safely, and will be secure without fear of evil."*

If your children listen to the wisdom of God's Word, they will do well. If you, as a parent, are instructing and training your children, throughout their lives, in God's Word, and they listen to you, they are going to do all right in life. If they do not listen to your instruction in God's wisdom, they will be in for some deep heartache.

Parents — do not get discouraged by this. Be faithful to God in training up your children and do not forget the promise God has given you in Proverbs 22:6, *"Train up a child in the way he should go, and when he is old he will not depart from it."*

You may (notice I said, "may" not "will") see your children rebel against you and God at some point in their lives. However, if you have been a godly parent, raising your children in the Word and being an example to them, they will return to the ways of the Lord. Do your part and trust the Lord to fulfill His Word!

Responsibility

We have talked a great deal about responsibility in this book. I have stressed how important it is for husbands, wives and parents to be responsible in the roles that God has given them. Just as it is important for parents to be responsible, it is equally important that parents teach their children to be responsible.

The Bible is very clear that we are to be responsible people. We are accountable for our actions and our behavior, and we need to be hard workers. There are numerous Scripture passages that teach about laziness and slothfulness.

Right from the beginning of their lives, your children need to be taught, not only to be responsible for their actions, but also for the effects of their actions on others. They need to be taught the responsibility of hard work. If your children, as they get older, are sitting around, sleeping late, being lazy and not helping around the house, but just living off of you — expecting that you, as the parent, will do everything for them — you have not taught them responsibility.

I did not grow up in a Christian home, however, I do remember being taught responsibility. Even when I was a kid, in grammar school, I cut lawns, washed cars and worked as a paper boy. I had my chores and as I got to my teen years, I worked as a box boy in a supermarket. If I chose to stay out late, as a teenager, my dad made sure I was up early the next morning to do my work around the house or get to my job. He was teaching me responsibility.

Many kids today do not know how to work. It is amazing, but you see, they have never been taught at home.

There are many young people not taking responsibility for their actions. In my day, if a boy got a girl pregnant, he did the responsible thing — he married her and took care of the girl and the baby. Today, young girls are being escorted to the abortion clinics, while their parents pay to have the baby aborted. The guy runs off scott free, leaving a girl traumatized and their baby dead. It is sinful — it is an abomination before the Lord.

What are you training your kids to be as adults? Are you teaching them to work hard so they can take care of themselves and their families, or are you teaching them that everything will be done for them? Are you teaching them to take responsibility for their actions, or are you teaching them to do as they please because you will bail them out of trouble, as you have always done?

Responsibility is an important matter that needs to begin when your children are young. Teach them to be responsible for what they say and do. Get them involved in things such as sports, church, clubs and activities. Do not allow your kids to sit and watch TV or play video games all day. Encourage them to play with other kids and do things as a family. When the children enter grammar school, give them chores. Teach them to pick up after themselves and do things that will help them have a good work ethic. Now, some parents go overboard on this and treat their kids as their own personal slaves. Use wisdom and show balance. Give them time to play. Make sure they do their homework!

Most importantly, be an example by being responsible yourself. Allow your children to see an example of a godly father, taking his responsibility as the leader and provider. Allow your children to see an example of a godly mother, as in Proverbs 31, who takes care of her family, home and work. If your children see irresponsibility and laziness in the home, then that is what they are going to be. Instill responsibility in your children — train them in this way, so they can mature into responsible adults, spouses and parents themselves.

Respect

"There is a generation that curses its father, and does not bless its mother" (Proverbs 30:11).

How many of you, as parents, are suffering in your own homes because your sons and daughters are physically or verbally abusing you? *"There is a generation…"* that is today's generation. Many young people do not respect their parents. Homes, today, are lacking in respect.

The fifth Commandment teaches children to *"Honor your father and your mother, that your days may be long upon the land which the Lord your God is giving you."* Yet, so often we see the opposite. It is amazing how rude some children are to their parents. I was in a grocery store one day and saw this kid, probably about ten years old, calling his mother "stupid." I felt like saying, "Hey kid, wake up." Where did he learn to call his mother "stupid?" Is Daddy calling her "stupid" at home?

I was in a clothing store with my wife the other day, and I was watching a teenage boy and his mother. He was probably 16 or 17 years old. The mother was trying to buy him some clothes and was giving him things to try on. This kid took some pants that his mother had given him and went to try them on. You could tell he did not want to do any of this. When he came out of the dressing room, he threw the pants right in his mother's face and cussed at her. This poor mother sat there and just kind of cowered and said, "Well, Honey...."

It is sad to see these types of things take place. Maybe you are in that kind of situation now. Well, you have to go back to the home. What have these children seen in the home? Does Dad do that to Mom? Does Mom do that to Dad?

Teaching your children respect starts with the husband and wife respecting each other. How can children respect their parents if the parents do not respect each other? This is so important. Begin by being an example in your home and take your children through the Scriptures that teach about respecting one another and respecting parental authority. They need to see this at an early age.

Deuteronomy 27:16 says, *"'Cursed is the one who treats his father or his mother with contempt.' And all the people shall say, 'Amen!'"*

The problem of disrespect in the home is not a new one. The Bible is filled with Scriptures regarding the issue of respect. In Proverbs 15:20 it says, *"A wise son makes a father glad, but a foolish man despises his mother."*

God wants peace in the home and this comes by teaching respect.

Parents, you need to see to it that you also respect your children. Ephesians 6:4 says, *"And you, fathers, do not provoke your children to wrath,…"* We will be touching upon this Scripture in the next section regarding discipline; however, I want to bring it to your attention now, because it is also speaking of respect. Parents do not make your children angry by the way you treat them. Do not tease your kids, tearing them down or embarrassing them in front of others. Respect them. Respect them in the same way you want to be respected by them. I have seen some parents rake their kids over the coals, and then they wonder why they do not have their respect.

Be an example. Respect one another and respect your kids. Train them in the way they should go by teaching them what God's Word says regarding respect. As you are obedient to God, you will see the fruit of your labor.

· · · 9 · · ·
Discipline Your Children In the Lord

Hebrews 12:9-11 tells us, *"Furthermore, we have had human fathers who corrected us, and we paid them respect. Shall we not much more readily be in subjection to the Father of spirits and live? For they indeed for a few days chastened us as seemed best to them, but He for our profit, that we may be partakers of His holiness. Now no chastening seems to be joyful for the present, but painful; nevertheless, afterward it yields the peaceable fruit of righteousness to those who have been trained by it."*

If God takes the time to chasten us for our own good, then should we not, as parents, take the time to correct and discipline our children for their good?

Notice, the above Scripture says chastening is a process of training, and the result is righteousness and peace. Webster's Dictionary defines *chastening* as, "to discipline in order to improve and correct." The Greek word for *chastening* is *paideia,* which means, "instruction, correction, nurture."

God wants us to correct our children. When they do something wrong, we need to sit down with them and explain that it is wrong and why.

We need to point out what the Scriptures say regarding the matter. Then, if you are going to punish them, share biblically why you are punishing them.

As parents, we need to understand that discipline is an act of love. In Proverbs 13:24 we read, *"He who spares his rod hates his son, but he who loves him disciplines him promptly."*

You need to discipline your children before they get to be teenagers. Many parents do not discipline their children while they are growing up, then the kids reach the rebellious teenage years and, suddenly, the parents are at a loss as to what to do. How can we spank a teenager? Why are my kids not listening to me? Why are they being so disobedient? As a parent, you need to begin the process of discipline when the children start walking — before habits or behaviors start to form.

How do you discipline?

Discipline involves admonition and chastening or punishment.

Admonition

Ephesians 6:4 tells us, *"And you, fathers, do not provoke your children to wrath, but bring them up in the training and admonition of the Lord."*

What does the word *admonition* refer to in this passage? It means to exhort. You are to take your children to the Scriptures. You are to teach them and guide them by the Word of God, correcting their behavior. Notice, though, the admonition is to be done in love, not in anger. God tells us first, as parents, do not provoke your children to wrath.

So many times, I am in a store somewhere and I see parents screaming and yelling at their kids. They are pulling them around harshly, speaking in anger to the point of harassment. The Bible is very clear about this — we are never to harass our children. We are never to discipline them in anger. When you provoke your children, you will arouse wrath in them and they will begin to hate you, as a parent. No, you need to lovingly discipline your children, because exhortation is a good thing when it is done in a loving manner.

Admonition means continually taking your children to the Scriptures when they have done something wrong. When your child speaks badly about somebody, take them to the passage that says, *"Do not speak evil of one another"* (James 4:11), or *"Bless those who curse you"* (Matthew 5:44). It is a continual process that begins when they are toddlers and continues throughout their teen years.

For example: "You know, Honey, in II Corinthians 6:14, the Bible says that you are not to be unequally yoked with a non-believer. Why? Because this is what happens."

"Son, in Proverbs 5, 6 and 7 it talks about the evil woman who will seduce you and take everything from you, leaving you with nothing."

The Bible is full of instruction for all of us. It is our manual on life. We need to use it when we are disciplining our children.

Another part of admonition is setting boundaries in the lives of your children.

How many homes do you know where the children do as they please? There are no rules — no boundaries. Maybe this is the condition of your home right now. Children must have boundaries and they must be clearly defined. Set rules for the home — be reasonable and let your children know that these boundaries are set up in love, for their protection and for their care. I have seen some parents go overboard and their house is a maze of do's and don'ts, based on legalism rather than God's grace. As a godly parent, seek the Lord's instruction and guidance in this matter, and do everything in a spirit of humility, grace and love. Then, your children will see your example and grow to know that Christianity is the Gospel of grace, not a legalistic and tireless religion. So many children rebel because their home was based on rules, regulations and legalism, not on God's wisdom, instruction, grace and love.

Chastening or Punishment

"To spank or not to spank," seems to be the question for so many today. Bookshelves are lined with books by psychologists who reason that spanking is a form of abuse and endangers the child mentally, as well as physically. How sad that this line of thinking has been transferred into the church of Jesus Christ.

Let me tell you, right now, there is nothing wrong with spanking. Spanking is sometimes a necessary form of discipline. The issue is how you spank your children, not whether you should or not.

Read Proverbs 13:24 again: *"He who spares his rod hates his son, but he who loves him disciplines him promptly."*

Do you know what the word *rod* means in Hebrew? It means "a branch or stick for correction." Now, do not get a stick and start beating your child. That is not what it says; however, I do believe that it means you should never use your hand to spank your child. Your hands are made for caressing. You hold your child's hands with yours, you use it to stroke them and you use your hand to brush their hair or wipe the tears from their eyes. Your child should not see your hand as an instrument of pain, fearing it every time you raise it. No, it is right to use a twig or a paddle instead.

So, how do you spank your child? Never spank your child in anger. You should sit down with your child and let them know why you are going to spank them, so they can learn and receive the discipline. When a spanking is administered in this way, though the child does not like it, they will learn from it and see that you love them. It is so important to spank in the right way, and, at times, it is equally important to spank at the right time. The Bible tells us if you spare the rod you will spoil the child. There are plenty of spoiled children in this world, who have never been corrected and disciplined.

Punishment serves as a means to show children that they must take responsibility for their behavior, and how wrong behavior has bad consequences. When punishment is left out of the discipline process, children begin to think and assume there are no consequences to their wrong behavior. If they are led to believe that wrong behavior has no bad consequences, they will continue to do what is wrong instead of what is right.

The Bible is very clear that we will reap what we sow. There are consequences to sinful behavior and, as parents, you need to clearly teach your kids this biblical truth.

There are other forms of punishment besides spanking, and these can be used in conjunction with, or rather than, spanking. Taking away a privilege for a specified period of time is one form of punishment. Again, be reasonable, humble and fair when you administer punishment — and always do it in love, praying with your child, so that resentment does not settle in their heart.

· · · 10 · · ·
Provide for Your Children's Well-Being

Of course, one of the most important aspects of being a parent is providing for your children's spiritual needs. We have spent a great deal of time discussing this important role.

There are two remaining important factors in raising your children. Parents must provide for both their physical and emotional well-being.

Physical

The most obvious physical needs a child has are food, clothing and shelter. It is tragic to read about the many children who grow up in motel rooms and tenements, where there is no running water, and the rooms are infested with cockroaches and rats. Most of the time, these same children have little clothing and suffer from malnutrition. How did they get in this position? Many of these children are by-products of single parents — many of them young kids themselves. Many of these children have been abandoned by their fathers, and many have parents who are strung out on drugs, spending whatever money they have on their drug addiction. There are also cases where the husband refuses to work, and so the family lives in squalor.

Parents are responsible to provide adequate shelter, clothing and food for their children. The Bible gives the primary role of providing for the family to the father. The Bible tells us, *"But if anyone does not provide for his own, and especially for those of his household, he has denied the faith and is worse than an unbeliever"* (1 Timothy 5:8).

The father's main concern and responsibility is to provide for the physical needs of his family. Today, many women are working, and though I feel it is best, when children are involved, for the mother to stay at home and take care of the children, it is for each couple to determine the woman's work schedule. However, the Bible remains the same, and the Lord NEVER directed the wife to be the provider — but the husband. In our economy today, it can be difficult for the family to rely on one income. However, I have seen, in many cases, the wife working because they have a higher standard of living, and so she has to work to help pay the car payments, etc. This is where parents need to use wisdom and deny their own selfish desires. God wants the husband to provide for the basic needs, and if you seek His will, He will open doors and give you wisdom to take care of your family.

Never sacrifice the needs of your children for non-necessities. Seek the Lord's direction and be diligent to obey His Word. Adequate physical provision and love go much further than luxury cars and upscale toys.

Emotional

A person's mental outlook and emotions are shaped in their childhood years. This is a delicate area and needs to be nurtured by God's Word and by the parent's tender loving care.

So many kids grow up in fear because they see constant turmoil, fighting and anger in the home, instead of acceptance, love and forgiveness. As a parent, you need to make sure your children feel secure in the home. It is never God's desire for children to be afraid — and it should never be a parent's desire either. A godly parent should want to foster a safe, peaceful and loving environment for their children. They need to know that you are watching out for them, protecting them and, most of all, loving them.

Be tender with your children, give them affection and let them know, verbally, that you love them. This goes a long way in establishing a healthy, emotional life. I have heard so many stories from adults who never had the attention, love and affection of their parents, when they were young. It can really mess up a person. God's love, of course, can heal these same adults; but how much better it is to raise your children in God's way, so they can become healthy adults.

In the same way, build up your child. Nothing is worse than a child trying desperately to get the approval of his parents. Encourage your children in their efforts; notice when they do something well, not just poorly. Find their strengths and promote them. Lift their spirits, give them the hope of the Gospel and always let them see that your attitude is one of humility, gentleness and kindness.

A Final Note . . .

Parenting is difficult, but it is also rewarding, and though the world mocks the role of parents, God esteems it. Nothing brings greater joy than to see your children walk with God.

You need to make the decision now — *". . . choose for yourselves this day whom you will serve, . ."* (Joshua 24:15a).

If you, as a spouse, have chosen to serve the Lord, then you can declare as a family, *"But as for me and my house, we will serve the Lord"* (Joshua 24:15 b). On the other hand, if you have chosen to serve yourself — your selfish desires, plans and ambitions — then your children will reap what you sow. Do not expect your children to walk with God, if you are not.

The question really is, "Who is influencing your family?"

I pray that the answer, in your home, is Jesus Christ!

Souls for Christ,

Raul

Scriptures to Help the Family

Husbands and Wives

Ephesians 5:17, 21-28, 33

"Therefore do not be unwise, but understand what the will of the Lord is. ... submitting to one another in the fear of God. Wives, submit to your own husbands, as to the Lord. For the husband is head of the wife, as also Christ is head of the church; and He is the Savior of the body. Therefore, just as the church is subject to Christ, so let the wives be to their own husbands in everything. Husbands, love your wives, just as Christ also loved the church and gave Himself for her, that He might sanctify and cleanse her with the washing of water by the Word, that He might present her to Himself a glorious church, not having spot or wrinkle or any such thing, but that she should be holy and without blemish. So husbands ought to love their own wives as their own bodies; he who loves his wife loves himself. Nevertheless let each one of you in particular so love his own wife as himself, and let the wife see that she respects her husband."

Titus 2:3-4

"...the older women likewise, that they be reverent in behavior, not slanderers, not given to much wine, teachers of good things — that they admonish the young women to love their husbands, to love their children,..."

Mothers and Fathers

Deuteronomy 6:6-7
"And these words which I command you today shall be in your heart. You shall teach them diligently to your children, and shall talk of them when you sit in your house, when you walk by the way, when you lie down, and when you rise up."

Deuteronomy 11:18-21
"Therefore you shall lay up these words of Mine in your heart and in your soul, and bind them as a sign on your hand, and they shall be as frontlets between your eyes. You shall teach them to your children, speaking of them when you sit in your house, when you walk by the way, when you lie down, and when you rise up. And you shall write them on the doorposts of your house and on your gates, that your days and the days of your children may be multiplied in the land of which the LORD swore to your fathers to give them, like the days of the heavens above the earth."

Deuteronomy 12:28
"Observe and obey all these words which I command you, that it may go well with you and your children after you forever, when you do what is good and right in the sight of the LORD your God."

Deuteronomy 32:46
"...and he said to them: 'Set your hearts on all the words which I testify among you today, which you shall command your children to be careful to observe — all the words of this law.'"

Psalms 127:3-5

"Behold, children are a heritage from the LORD, The fruit of the womb is a reward. Like arrows in the hand of a warrior, So are the children of one's youth. Happy is the man who has his quiver full of them; They shall not be ashamed, But shall speak with their enemies in the gate."

Proverbs 19:18

"Chasten your son while there is hope, And do not set your heart on his destruction."

Proverbs 22:6

"Train up a child in the way he should go, And when he is old he will not depart from it."

Proverbs 29:17

"Correct your son, and he will give you rest; Yes, he will give delight to your soul."

Matthew 19:13-15

"Then little children were brought to Him that He might put His hands on them and pray, but the disciples rebuked them. But Jesus said, 'Let the little children come to Me, and do not forbid them; for of such is the kingdom of heaven.' And He laid His hands on them and departed from there."

2 Corinthians 12:14b
"For the children ought not to lay up for the parents, but the parents for the children."

Ephesians 6:4
"And you, fathers, do not provoke your children to wrath, but bring them up in the training and admonition of the Lord."

Colossians 3:21
"Fathers, do not provoke your children, lest they become discouraged."

1 Timothy 3:4-5
"...one who rules his own house well, having his children in submission with all reverence (for if a man does not know how to rule his own house, how will he take care of the church of God?);"

Children

Proverbs 1:7-9
"The fear of the LORD is the beginning of knowledge, But fools despise wisdom and instruction. My son, hear the instruction of your father, And do not forsake the law of your mother; For they will be a graceful ornament on your head, And chains about your neck."

Proverbs 3:1-6

"My son, do not forget my Law, But let your heart keep my commands; For length of days and long life And peace they will add to you. Let not mercy and truth forsake you; Bind them around your neck, Write them on the tablet of your heart, And so find favor and high esteem In the sight of God and man. Trust in the LORD with all your heart, And lean not on your own understanding; In all your ways acknowledge Him, And He shall direct your paths."

Ephesians 6:1-3

"Children, obey your parents in the Lord, for this is right. 'Honor your father and mother,' which is the first commandment with promise: 'that it may be well with you and you may live long on the earth.'"

I Timothy 5:8

"But if anyone does not provide for his own [parents], and especially for those of his household, he has denied the faith and is worse than an unbeliever."

THE DYNAMICS
OF LEVERAGE

*12 UNWRITTEN INFLUENCE RULES
FOR LEADERSHIP, LIFE, & LUNCH*

G'SEAN WILLIAMS, CPSM

First paperback edition March 2020

ISBN 978-1-7347441-1-8

Edited by: Katrina J. Rivera
Edited by: Angela Taylor

Book Cover Design by: SMS Advisors
www.SMS-Advisors.com

Published by PSM Training Solutions, LLC
www.PSMTrainingSolutions.com

Snapshot About the Author

G'Sean Williams, CPSM is a global procurement & supply management trainer, industry speaker, and experienced international business-to-business negotiator. Over the last 20 years, he has negotiated over $1.5 Billion USD in contracts with hundreds of small businesses and Fortune 1000 suppliers in over 15 regions across the world. In the last 8 years, he has also led capacity building and growth efforts of over 80 small businesses leveraging his foundation of negotiating and writing contracts for many multi-billion-dollar global organizations.

Born and raised on the tough streets of Detroit, G'Sean avoided drugs and gangs to excel as the Class President of Henry Ford High School. He went on to study Supply Chain Management and graduated from Michigan State University where he started to expand and accelerate his exposure to world culture, music, religion, and leadership.

In 2012, his mother was diagnosed with cancer and his nephew was shot and killed on those same streets of Detroit. On the path to reaching the corporate vice president level by his late 30's, G'Sean took an unprecedented leave of absence to focus on family. G'Sean made a critical decision to move his mother to a natural supplement regiment to reduce the side effects of chemotherapy. Risking her life, she immediately went into 100% remission.

With only months left of his corporate leave after his mother's recovery, he took partnership in a boutique procurement training organization and the challenge to grow it to a half-million-dollar practice. Along this journey, he gained adjunct instructor status at 5 top-tier universities and partnered with many chambers of commerce organizations and the US Small Business Administration to share his knowledge with corporate professionals and small business leaders across the United States.

After designing new and innovative leadership development initiatives and training programs for the industry, he was invited to do it globally. This popularity led to the delivery of leadership training programs for thousands of professionals in North America, Central America, Europe, Southeast Asia, and the Middle East. It was then that G'Sean created and developed Personal Negotiation Styles, The Six Dynamics of Influence, and Influence Techniques as reference tools to help professionals in the Procurement & Supply Chain industry master their craft.

His small business clients realized that these concepts were great for the profession, but also applicable to small business leaders even more. With entrepreneurs frequently being forced to balance business and life, G'Sean realized that the same skill sets he taught to thousands of corporate leaders and entrepreneurs, were universally applicable to ordinary navigation of life and relationships.

For speaking engagement booking, leadership coaching, or corporate training scheduling, please contact SMS Advisors @ 704.503.9103 or email info@sms-advisors.com

PSMTrainingSolutions.com

Contents

CHAPTER 1 - *Power of Realization* 1

CHAPTER 2 – *Embracing That Lil Style of Yours* 15

CHAPTER 3 – *Letting Your Style Shine* 23

CHAPTER 4 – *Six Dynamics of Influence* 29

CHAPTER 5 – *Carving ROCK Solid Deals!* 41

CHAPTER 6 – *Showing the Money* 55

CHAPTER 7 – *Is Everything Negotiable?* 65

CHAPTER 8 – *Perfection Prides Preparation!* 71

CHAPTER 9 – *Negotiating with the Crew* 85

CHAPTER 10 – *Balancing Leverage Philosophies* 97

CHAPTER 11 – *Don't Sweat Their Technique* 103

CHAPTER 12 – *Influential Leverage for Lunch* 123

CHAPTER 1

Power of Realization

For some, having influence is rewarding. For some, having influence is powerful. For others, it often doesn't matter because they rarely seem to be able to influence big outcomes at work or in life when it matters the most. Influence is an art form that could determine the ease or struggle of your quest for leadership, your journey to master everyday life, or simply your mission to conquer lunch with colleagues. For most, the art of influence manifests when it's time for an overdue promotion, convincing their significant other to clean out that cluttered garage, or when their manager wants to grab a greasy pizza for lunch with them while they are trying to stick to a new diet. No one is exempt from needing this essential life skill although most people fear the clarity, criticism, and potential conflict which comes along with it sometimes.

If you happen to be like me, you thrive on clarity, criticism, and productive conflict for a living. Like millions of others across the globe, I negotiate deals for a living. I am a procurement professional. Working side by side with corporate attorneys, we facilitate the deal and focus on commercial and operational activities while our attorney friends focus on legalities.

Do you remember the movie, "*Jerry McGuire*?" It's about a brash athlete (played by Cuba Gooding, Jr) who wants the best in life for himself and his family. Ok, maybe he's a little flashy and wants a little more than his fair share mainly due to his aging body and somewhat dwindling performance on the field. Nevertheless, he is represented by an up and coming sports agent (played by Tom Cruise) who decided to create his own sports agency. His new empire represents athletes who may desire better contract payouts than deserved. Tom Cruise's character, Jerry

Maguire, was the savior for Cuba Gooding, Jr's character, Rod Tidwell, who had at least a little juice left in the squeeze. The movie was a big hit in the mid-nineties and earned Gooding an Oscar.

If you can imagine that environment or recall the movie, then you have a snapshot into the world of the procurement professional and how we work as a contract agent for corporations. Although, most times the deals are not as dramatic. However, we're a group of professionals hired to represent stakeholders, negotiate deals, develop contracts, and ultimately spend trillions of dollars for the corporations, government agencies, and small businesses we represent. I'll eventually tell you how I stumbled into the world of influence, who made the unlikely introduction, and the valuable life lessons I learned along my journey.

For now, let me paint the picture of the event that sparked me to start writing a book. In 2009, I was recruited to work for a large pharmaceutical company in New Jersey. I was responsible for how we spent $575 million USD a year and choosing our suppliers.

In this new and exciting role, I represented a group of stakeholders (or internal customers) who were responsible for operating our buildings and facilities worldwide. This included securing our campuses, cleaning our windows and offices, ensuring employees had heat and water, preparing and serving food in the cafeterias, managing the gyms and childcare facilities, etc. It's like running a city inside of a city. If you could think of something you needed as an employee of our company to make you more comfortable during your workday, my global stakeholders and procurement team collaborated and negotiated with suppliers to make it happen.

I was five or six months into my role when I took an assignment to meet with 20 or so folks involved with an enterprise-wide project to negotiate a deal worth $865 million USD. At the time, I am only about 10 years into this procurement & supply chain career. I am still relatively fresh out of Michigan State University and excited about conquering the everyday art of influence - both the good and the bad! The good being working externally with amazing supplier partners and being a part of their multi-million-dollar growth stories when they performed well. The bad being the unforeseen internal struggles with "out of sync" leaders, distracted colleagues, and poor-performing direct reports which seemed to come along with the job.

Nevertheless, that moment in Rome changed me. I've negotiated hundreds of millions of dollars here at home and abroad before I was 30. At the same time, some of my college friends were still living at home with their parents trying to figure out life. Some of my childhood friends from Gilchrist Street in Detroit, MI, were still caught in the claws of inner city poverty looking for the next hustle or part-time job to get by. Meanwhile, I was having life-changing experiences in countries I've only seen on TV or a world globe in grade school.

Among these life-changing experiences, I never could have guessed that one day soon I would experience an event that would forever change the way I looked at the concept of influential leverage. It would transcend my way of dealing with family, friends, strangers, colleagues or anyone I was personally or professionally working with. It adjusted the way I saw the energy of people, the motives behind their actions, or their means of maneuvering in unfavorable situations.

This trip to Italy involved a project in which the negotiations were so complex that the initial concept of consolidating these efforts globally had been evaluated for years before I even got to the company. As the new Head of Global Facilities Procurement for a $22 billion USD corporation, I am only briefed from my team that a group will be waiting for my timely arrival in Rome to move the project forward and finalize the scope. My flight into Rome was delayed and my only option, once I landed, was to shower at the airport and take a car directly to our manufacturing facility where the meeting was held.

On a side note, the showers in the airline concierge lounge are usually amazing. As a kid from Detroit, I never thought I would be taking showers in secret airline clubs at international airports.

Nevertheless, with a fresh shower and car service waiting, I finally arrived at our facility about 45 minutes west of Rome. By the time I got there, the meeting participants were in the conference room exchanging pleasantries and awaiting my arrival to formally get started. When I walked into the lobby, I am greeted by Roberto. He is a charismatic Italian on my extended team who was responsible for orchestrating this meeting. Although a global initiative, my US-based centralized procurement team was ultimately responsible for the final procurement recommendation. Roberto and I have strategized over the phone many times; however, this is my first time meeting him face-to-face as we walk through the hallways of his plant which I've never been before. For that matter, I realized that I have never conducted business in Rome before either. This is all new! At that moment it hit me. I had no idea who the people were in this conference room Roberto and I were speed walking towards. Fear of the unknown starts to settle in my stomach. I'm surprised it hasn't already before this point. I guess some people fear what they don't know, and others fear what they do know.

On the last stretch of the walk, Roberto briefs me that we have a large group in the room. He confirms it's a mixed crowd of company folks and key supplier folks. In addition to that, our team and the suppliers represented multiple European regions.

And then boom! Before I can think of any last-minute comfort questions, brainstorm eleventh-hour preparation, or find a reason to delay this pending grand entrance, he says, "Look who's here!" as we breach the threshold to an open-door "state of the art" conference room. Eyes were glaring and necks were bending to get a first glance at the man whose bio has gone out to the entire company as the new Head of Global Facilities Procurement.

I looked around the room, with what I am sure was a glossed over daze, and I see faces from all different nationalities. As they say, "Hello" in English, I hear native tongues from at least Ireland, Italy, Spain, France, and maybe a couple of other places I couldn't identify at the time. I am all of 30 or 31 years old and this global influence thing just got real!

After sitting down and getting settled, I realized that the table-top surface in front of me looked empty and I gave folks across the table clear line of sight to my mental control center. One thing I learned early in my career is to never force yourself to master influence in an uncomfortable environment.

Rule #1: If you aren't feeling your situation, feel free to change the vibe or the venue.

For example, let's say you don't want to talk to your "short attention span" manager in their office with people in and out. However, you need to discuss the promotion you deserve before finishing an application to enroll your kids in a much better school next year. You can change the "venue" and possibly the "vibe" by asking your boss if you can catch them on the way out at the end of the day. Make sure to pick a day in which you've learned your boss is headed to their star-athlete son's soccer tournament. Getting them out of their office, you have changed the "venue." With family on their mind, you have changed the "vibe" of the discussion to make it easier to level-set on how important family is to you. In fact, both of you!

Bringing it back to Rome, I slightly altered my venue by quickly pulling out my company-issued laptop. I placed it right in front of me and opened it up just like at my desk in the office. Perfect! It was like a safety blanket providing me with a shield over my chest to those directly across the table from me. Small mental victories are still victories, right?

Roberto, now sitting to my immediate right, made a great and timely suggestion as I marveled at my brash decision to defend my territory with the laptop shield move. He said, "Why don't we all go ahead and introduce ourselves." This is brilliant because I honestly had no idea who was on my team, "Spend Money" vs. the supplier team, "Get Money." Everyone took turns introducing themselves and briefly speaking to what they thought of this huge project so far, both pros and cons.

There was only one problem. Through the international accents and acronyms, some of both which I've never heard at this point in my life, I still don't know who works for my company and who is representing the supplier. I remember thinking, "This is going to be interesting!" At this moment I realized something so profound and critical to my future drive to master influence, both in leadership and in life. This moment changed my view and hence my ability to better influence decisions and outcomes. Now, I much more enjoy pursuing all types of influence victories from free hotel room upgrades to my continuous pursuit of global dominance as the Greatest Businessman Ever. Just joking! Sometimes I am too tired after long flights to negotiate free upgrades; however, the Greatest Businessman Ever is always in the works. 😊

So, what did I realize in Rome? I noticed that before and as people speak, most can't help but pass back and forth internal messages between their mind, eyes, lips, arms, hands, legs, and feet. It is almost like a trapdoor of communication or a secret society of intellectual combat happening right in everyone's line of sight. I realized everyone (well mostly everyone) thinks before they speak, and they further express true intentions in eye contact, timely vocal inflection, body language, and gestures of physical touch. Like a pat on the shoulder as your boss is telling you he is looking out for you during promotion time.

With this new theory to ponder and observe, I realized that it is not safe to assume those closest to you are always on your team. I always felt all my colleagues wanted the same success for our company. We all "bleed the same company blood" right? I was wrong! Some of them would secretly wish for the project to be a failure to ensure their vested interest.

Rule #2: Always know the people you are dealing with and the things which motivate them to deal with you.

To get to the truth of people and their motives or to just learn to size up the room quickly, the first step is to understand people. I know that is vague.

However, we can streamline knowing people by understanding their typical disposition, their current situation, and how both of those are relative to their reason for dealing with you. I call this "Preliminary Motive Pulling." This concept I created was born from understanding who wanted what and why at that table in Rome and I've been using it for leveraging influence ever since.

Sometimes what people say reveals what they believe. However, it's often either confirmed or contradicted by what they do before, during, and after they speak. We must patiently observe their behavior. People tend to remove the filter when they just turned in their notice for a much better gig or find themselves on the verge of getting fired. We all remember Craig's journey when he got fired on Friday, his day off. If not, google it!

Nevertheless, if people are not motivated to deal with you sincerely, often-times their words and their actions may not align completely in these comfortable or stressful environments. Being able to pre-identify this in the first, second, or even the third interaction could save a lot of time and energy in your leadership quest. Not to mention this skill will save you a lot of time and emotional heartbreak in life as well. Lastly, it may help you decide who is and who is not worth having lunch with.

We can dedicate an entire book to this concept of "Preliminary Motive Pulling" as the starting point of influence but that sounds like another bestseller idea. For now, this concept helps us focus and better understand the people around us who we deal with. However, before we focus our attention completely on the people we deal with, we must work harder to understand our style and its potential origins.

CHAPTER 2
Embracing That Lil Style of Yours

Growing up in the inner city of Detroit, you don't get many real-life chances to see corporate executives negotiating in all-glass conference rooms with a 30th-floor panorama view of the city like on an episode of "Scandal." With that backdrop, my introduction to influence and eventually my career came from a reliable source that was a little closer to home than you would think. It was one of the most powerful women I've ever encountered who probably never held a gun in her life. The most powerful example of negotiation and influence in my early childhood was all 5'3" or maybe even 5'2" of my mother!

I first remember her in action at Northland Mall in our hometown. It was the late eighties in the era when JC Penney, Hudson, and Sears ruled the shopping experience. Amazon wasn't even born yet! During this time, there was no such thing as a retail kiosk in the middle of the mall. You were either a storefront or not. In the middle of the mall, you pretty much got an option of green plants for scenery or hard bench chairs for those battled-wounded spouses ready to give up the good fight and have a sit-down. Speaking of giving up the good fight, my mother had this favorite store called Winkelman's which seemed to be my second home. My life at the age of 11 or 12 consisted of home, school, church, and Winkelman's.

Nevertheless, in some sort of rare retribution to her only son for those endless evenings in Winkelman's, we ended up in a KB Toy Store. For those of you who never heard of KB Toy Store... it's ok! Imagine stuffing Toys"R"Us within a 40-foot storefront mall slot and removing over half the toys and voilà! If you have never heard of Toys"R"Us, imagine if Amazon did a small pop up shop for toys inside of a Chick-fil-A. If you haven't heard of Amazon, I took way too long to finish this book or my family is still receiving royalties in the 25th century.

Anyway, so I'm roaming the aisle aimlessly at KB Toy Store picking a toy that I could maneuver into the "on the fly" budget for my mother's approval. Whoa (in my Joey from *"Blossom"* voice)!! There it is, a Super Soaker! What is a Super Soaker some may ask? Only the best water gun ever invented. The only problem with the plan to push this transaction through is there is no price to be found on the Super Soaker or the rack I pulled it from. There are prices listed for everything else I'm not interested in. Even obviously much more inferior water guns. So, I remembered a couple of prices of the cheaper water pistols and proceeded to report out to my mother for the ultimate decision on the Super Soaker that I may or may not truly know the real price. She says ok!

We get to the counter and just as I expected, no one knows what the real price is! Three minutes, four minutes, five minutes of "price checking" go by and my chances of making this transaction happen are getting slim. I call this pending moment the "IWO" or "Influence Window of Opportunity." Instead of the window getting shut, I am getting ready to experience the brilliance of my mother and I didn't even know it was coming. It started very simply with, "This is ridiculous." I later learned this was one of my mother's favorite "go-to" lines before her telling someone a little more about themselves. I don't mean like a corporate retreat icebreaker "more about yourself." I mean like a mess with a woman's child, "more about yourself!"

She followed that grand opening by saying, "Do you know how long we have been standing here waiting for someone to figure out the price of this toy? We have been very patient letting people cut in front of us, but now this is getting ridiculous." At this time, as the line is now getting longer and longer, the manager was summoned from the back. My mother went on to let her know out of all the water guns they had back there that "it is a failure in your process to not have this type of thing figured out where we are not inconvenienced as the customer." Even at a young age, I observed this young manager feeling the pressure of the spotlight on her and the long line forming. Not being able to change her "vibe" or the "venue" we discussed earlier, I guess the manager decided that getting my mother out of her store by any means would be the best move for her and her sanity. It was then that the manager said softly to the register clerk, "just pick our cheapest water gun and ring them up for that price. It's fine!" Wow! I will never really know how much that Super Soaker cost, but I'm assuming it was more than $2.99 USD.

My mother was famous or infamous depending on what side of the table you were on regarding the next rule.

Rule #3: If all else fails, call out their process flaws to enhance your leverage.

Over the years I have learned how to perform Process Failure Mode and Effects Analysis or PFMEA's. This is an exercise in which you process map activity and possible failures in the order in which those actions may occur. You then identify areas in advance where that activity could breakdown due to people, systems, or procedural errors. For example, let's practice on your very busy but extremely frugal significant other who loves opening your house to their family. Let's say they have been delaying in putting up those new shelves you bought from Target weeks ago. You may decide to informally perform this influence process and not even be aware of what you are doing. You start by asking them what they think about spending money to bring in a handyman to put those shelves up on the wall. You then emphasize how busy you know they are at work and that you only want to get those shelves done quickly so you can focus on finishing the living room decorations for their mother's upcoming visit. If that doesn't get them, you then double down and suggest that it's ok if they wait until the last minute to put them up only if they don't mind helping you decorate as well. You are almost done. After letting them marinate on OPTIONS, not ULTIMATUMS, you then give them a final out by telling them you found a few low-cost handymen with excellent reviews.

Giving options for closure and being in tune with what your significant other is capable and not capable of doing allows you to leverage and influence the discussions and outcomes better. When you make it their idea to go ahead and hire a handyman or let them conclude they don't want to help you with decorations during their favorite TV show or football game, congrats! Game. Set. Match!

Some people reading this will fully embrace the approach and start to think about the "shelves" and what they represent in your life. Others will feel like it's easier to just tell their significant other to put up the shelves or else! Others will just decide to pay for someone to put them up and deal with their complaining spouse later claiming that they were "just about to do it and we didn't need to spend that money." Others would go ahead and start putting the shelves up themselves and may or may not get angrier at their significant other every five minutes that pass and they don't offer to help. Others may say screw the shelves and the upcoming visit altogether, especially if you never liked their mother.

Regardless of how you are wired, we will explore your potential Personal Negotiation Style and Six Dynamics of Influence in Chapters 3 and 4 to support your quest to conquer leadership, life, and lunch.

CHAPTER 3
Letting Your Style Shine

Walking out of the toy store with a new Super Soaker in my hand, Personal Negotiation Styles became a loose concept to me. I would try to read people and understand their style every chance I got. I would fascinate myself by exploring the reason why some people in my family were comfortable standing in front of everyone and voicing their opinion and others were more soft-spoken but calculating in their approach to influencing others in private discussions. For years I observed and informally studied family, friends, colleagues, and strangers!

It wasn't until years later in 2014 that I decided I wanted to do something more formal. Equipped with 14 years of negotiating experience from closing billions of dollars of contracts with suppliers and opportunities to deal with people from all walks of life, I wanted to formally track the Personal Negotiation Styles and Influence Techniques of professionals in different regions around the world. For four years, my company and I educated and studied business professionals of all ages, backgrounds, and parts of the world. Dealing with mostly Americans and Europeans during my corporate career, I now expanded my understanding of these concepts to Asia. We extended the "Influential Leverage" study another 2 years and learned Central American and Middle Eastern cultures more closely. On this journey, I learned there are two main types of Personal Negotiation Styles and four subcategories. At a high-level, it's obvious when I'm dealing with a leader who is a Negotiation Hunter versus a leader who is a Negotiation Gatherer.

Negotiation   Hunters   -   In   Summary
Negotiation Hunters enjoy the smell of victory more so in the thick of negotiation delivery. They pride themselves on the results. They usually always plan and remember creativity in their negotiation approach. However, a structured process is optional. Negotiation Hunters like to grab the attention of the audience and appear very comfortable with ambiguity for the most part. Sometimes part of their strategy is to create ambiguity. If given talking points and only minutes to prepare, Negotiation Hunters can make people feel like any topic was well studied. Negotiation Hunters "copy and paste" ideas from the "world" and are very good outsourcing or quickly gathering research to back up their delivery and approach.

Negotiation   Gatherers   -   In   Summary
Negotiation Gatherers enjoy the smell of victory more so in the calm of strategizing and they love team caucuses for ultimate synchronization. They pride themselves on free-flowing information exchange and

the strength of their team's preparation. They remember key moments well and a structured negotiation process ensures their brilliance. Negotiation Gatherers strongly prefer clear upfront missions as opposed to a lot of ambiguity and will earn teammates' trust with their attention to detail. When given direction and ample time to prepare, Negotiation Gatherers can formulate the data or facts to look how it needs to look to help them and teammates win the negotiation. Negotiation Gatherers like quick feedback from the team and seek examples from the "world" to validate their detailed research and findings. Whether a Negotiation Hunter or Negotiation Gatherer, there are levels to each one.

Graphic 2.1

Which one are you? One way to get a better understanding of yourself and others is to understand what motivates you and how you interact with others. If you are closer to being 100 percent driven by results and delivery, you are most likely a Negotiation Hunter. If you are about results and delivery and find it easier to get things done by yourself because you oftentimes are the only person who knows exactly what it takes, you may be higher up on the Negotiation Hunter side of the graphic. If you are closer to being 100 percent driven by steps and structure, you are most likely a Negotiation Gatherer. If you are about steps and structure and you ultimately prefer to create reports and shape the data for other people to do all of the talking during negotiations, you are most likely higher up on the Negotiation Gathering side of the graphic. If you are further down on the graphic on either side, you may be more collaborative and may from time to time collaborate a little too much. For example, giving way too many options for lunch spots on a date.

Either way, leaders come in all styles and a diversity of styles creates balance in the workplace and within personal relationships. In our on-site corporate training programs, we found strong correlations to the strengths and weaknesses of a team's ability to influence decisions enterprise-wide and the balance of Negotiation Hunters and Gatherers in the group.

Whether, in leadership or life, both Negotiation Hunters and Negotiation Gatherers often find ways to leverage the Six Dynamics of Influence to gain influence. These styles and influences start to bring the dynamics of leverage to life!

Want to learn more about your Personal Negotiation Style? Go to:

http://bit.ly/PERSONALNEGOTIATIONSTYLES

CHAPTER 4
Six Dynamics of Influence

Have you ever wondered why some people are easily influenced, while others are not? Maybe you often struggle with motivating your colleagues, your children, or a stubborn parent who refuses to realize why that smartphone is so smart. I often wonder what motivates some people to take on entrepreneurship and some to leave at 4:59 pm every day from their 8-5 job.

As we developed Personal Negotiation Styles and taught the concept around the world, we also stumbled into six visible and consistent dynamics which we observed professionals use to help them influence others during our simulated negotiation exercises. We were shocked to see these reoccurring dynamics work consistently across the Middle East, Central America, North America, and Asia. The Six Dynamics of Influence we saw are PRIZE, PROMISE, PLACE, POSTURE, PROCESS, and PROTOTYPE.

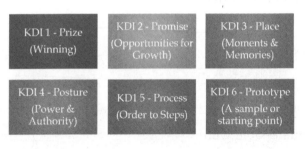

Graphic 4.1

I will take the time to explain each one. First, let's lay a ground-rule. Just because you may be influenced and motivated by one or two particular Dynamics of Influence, it is not a guarantee that someone you are trying to positively influence is also driven by those same Dynamics of Influence. You would need to understand their Personal Negotiation Style, mentioned in Chapter 3, and Negotiation Approaches

& Leverage Philosophies discussed in Chapter 10 to have more insight. Remember, not all people are wired to think like you, unfortunately! So, let's cover those Six Key Dynamics of Influence individually.

KDI 1 – PRIZE: You probably guessed it. The Prize Dynamic of Influence is about winning! Some people are wired to win. It's not that they want the other person or team to always lose. They just desire to feel the accomplishment of being right and rewarded more. The reward comes in many different forms. Some people would say money is a form and that is correct. However, there is more depth to Prize. In addition to money, a prize could also be a promotion, a card for your birthday, free bikes offered at your hotel for no cost, or identifying a shortcut home to save five minutes. In my profession, a lot of us focus on cost savings as our prize. If we are paying $5 million USD for something, we would always rather pay $4.5 million USD because it is rewarding.

When I worked for a large semiconductor company in the US Pacific Northwest, I volunteered to do corporate recruiting at Michigan State University (Go Green!) for up and coming procurement & supply chain talent. I would fly into Detroit and drive to East Lansing which is only 90 minutes away. This made it easier to return the rental car for work and rent another car to see family in Detroit for the weekend. In doing this multiple times a year, for years, I never understood why my father got so offended when I rented a car. One year I started paying more attention and then it hit me. *The cheaper I told my father I rented the car for or the better the deal I got from the car rental company, the more acceptable me renting a car was to him.* I realized in this situation, my father was influenced by Prize and his version of personal cost savings. He was ok with me renting a car only if I got a better deal than everyone else who rented cars. Although this was his position on me renting cars to visit family in Detroit, Prize wasn't his Dynamic of Influence for everything. So, be careful because people may have different Dynamics of Influence applicable in different situations. However, everyone usually has one or two default Dynamics of Influence they fall victim to or leverage when a situation is extremely comfortable or stressful.

KDI 2 – PROMISE: I mentioned the movie *"Jerry McGuire"* earlier and speaking of athletes, I was an athlete myself. Unfortunately, I wasn't that good or else I would be retired somewhere on my yacht in the South of France wondering if my ghostwriter finished that book on influence that we discussed.

Nevertheless, I recall attending a basketball camp in high school where recruiters would pull talented players to the side in the hallway and discuss their potential. It seemed like coaches, scouts, players, and families were all driven by the Promise Dynamic of Influence. Promise is embedded in the potential to win the tournament, the potential to recruit the next Michael Jordan, the potential to start at the next level, or the potential for your son or daughter to get a free ride at an amazing university like Michigan State (Go White!). Regardless of the motivation, the number one Dynamic of Influence at that basketball camp, and mostly all sports camps for that matter, was Promise.

Again, Promise is based on the belief that you or the person you are dealing with will often prioritize opportunities for growth. This could be the positioning for a promotion, being considered for more business by a client, being put on the waitlist for first-class, the potential of being the next new internet sensation, or the idea that the next one is the one. If the thrill of the journey drives you more than the ultimate Prize than you are most likely driven by the Promise. Being driven by Promise could be healthy as long as you or loved ones are not being taken advantage of while along for the ride.

KDI 3 – PLACE: Do you remember that one time at band camp when everyone decided to sneak out of the dorm one night? If you do and are willing to do it again because of how good it felt to be free, then the Place Dynamic of Influence has your name all over it. For me, it was 1990. The score was 90-90 as the Detroit Pistons were playing the Portland Trailblazers at home for the NBA Championship. It was 20.1 seconds on the clock and the Pistons were coming out of the time-out ready to execute the play drawn up from Chuck Daly.

I even think Dennis Rodman had a normal haircut and maybe only one tattoo as he inbounded the ball from the sideline. He passed it to Isiah Thomas, and it was almost a guarantee Isiah would shake and bake to get to the rim. Isiah penetrated and suddenly stopped to pass the ball to Vinnie Johnson. Vinnie Johnson was known as VJ, but his name would forever change at this moment. Why? Because he was destined to become named Double O7 as he took one or two dribbles and launched the game-winning shot with nothing but 00.7 left on the clock! Why does this matter?

Fast forward to 2007 when a colleague was trying to influence me to go in with him on season tickets for the Washington Wizards. We were working in Richmond, VA which was easily 90 minutes away from the arena, and possibly more than two hours with traffic. It wasn't the price or the opportunity to revive my hoop dreams which got me on board. It was reliving those moments and memories with my family and friends. Those memories that I felt with my mother and sisters sitting in the living room watching

00.7 drop that last-second shot to win the 1990 NBA Championship 17 years prior. Season tickets would put me back in that "Place" and for two years family and I would watch many game-winning shots from 15 rows away.

KDI 4 – POSTURE: Remember when your parents used to tell you to do something and you had the nerve to ask why? Or maybe your kids now have the nerve to ask you why? The famous default answer for some household leaders was "because I told you so." What about when your mother came out on the porch when it started getting dark and just stood there. You automatically knew it was time to tell your friends good-bye. If you had that experience, have friends who had that experience, or stood out on your porch last night to signal your kid to come on home, then you are most likely familiar with Posture. Essentially, it's an expression, tone of voice, body language, and/or a gesture that is meant to demonstrate real or perceived power and leverage.

The Posture Dynamic of Influence is used in personal relationships and dating to establish parameters, especially in the early stages. Have you ever made an unwelcome attempt to touch a black girl's hair in the nineties? If you have, you most likely remember the Posture look you got. How about those two weeks of walking around your office at work with your head held high after you turned in your resignation for a much better job? You were Posturing. In negotiations, people influence and are influenced by Posture because it symbolizes power and authority!

KDI 5 – PROCESS: You can find anything on YouTube, right? As a consultant and educator, the summertime is usually slower than other times of the year, so it's a great time for seeing family, taking a vacation, and signing up for things you have no business doing. It sounds a lot like retirement now that I put it that way. Nevertheless, one day I was driving, and my check engine light came on in my car. After a check engine diagnostic, I got a price of $950 USD to replace a mass air sensor in my car. Before I authorized the repair, I decided to check around and see how much the actual part cost. To my surprise, the part was only $132 USD. I immediately evaluated the scope, schedule, and benefit. I had plenty of time and I could save a lot of money relatively speaking. The only thing I didn't have was scope. How exactly do I accomplish this repair on a moderately complex car?! You got it. YouTube! I googled how to do this repair and I found an amazing step-by-step video. I was motivated to go for it with the Process support of YouTube.

People who are influenced by Process usually appreciate a good checklist or structured approach. They understand that everything has a pre-requisite, a sequence, and an outcome. If you find yourself negotiating with someone influenced by Process, make sure to have attention to detail and logical order for your discussion. Lastly, if you are looking for a good mechanic, I got a guy.

KDI 6 – PROTOTYPE: The last one is simple. "Seeing is believing." Some people can't be influenced until they can literally see what you are talking about. I noticed that the easiest way to convince someone on my leadership team in Corporate America to do something is to share with them how one of our competitors was doing it. For small business owners, it could be about sharing with a client that you have done certain programs with other companies in their industry.

Personally, Prototype occurs often in our quest for love and family. A lot of people don't know exactly what the perfect person or family for them looks like until they encounter or meet them. If this is or was the case for you, there is a good chance your experiences over the years subconsciously built a Prototype for you to measure others against.

Overall, remember people may be influenced by any of the Six Dynamics of Influence based on their Personal Negotiation Style, as well as, the current situation they may be in. However, most people may have two default Dynamics of Influence which they may leverage, as well as, be leveraged by consistently. If someone has great intentions, encourage the sharing of your primary Dynamics of Influences for a better relationship. However, be careful not to make it too easy for people with mischievous or unknown intentions to learn how to manipulate you with access to this same information.

Understanding these dynamics in your daily interactions will come in handy for leadership opportunities, quality of life, or a really good free lunch. However, closing a deal doesn't always mean it is a good deal. Next, let's explore exactly what a ROCK solid deal looks like and how we use the model as a check and balance for influencing others during simple or complex negotiations.

CHAPTER 5
Carving ROCK Solid Deals!

If you are like most people, you love a good checklist. Even for those of us who play by our own rules and tend to march to our own drum, it's nice to see a checklist from time to time to make life easier.

Rule #4: Make sure your deals are "ROCK" solid to avoid buyer's remorse.

Some years ago, in my mid-twenties, I was enjoying my time traveling across North America and Europe procuring all types of lumber and fibers which go into mattresses. Yes, that thing we sleep on every night but only care about what's inside of it once every seven years or so. In this global procurement role at an international mattress manufacturer, I learned so much about what makes a mattress and how important that combination was for a quality night of sleep. However, I get no commission for selling mattresses so back to how this relates to the dynamics of leverage and Rule #4.

One day I was sitting in the office and I got a call from one of our 21 manufacturing plants, right next door to our corporate office. The buyer told me about all the issues they were having with one of our suppliers. Unfortunately, only three months into the job, I just inherited all of these contract agreements which I hadn't even had time to read yet, let alone give guidance on some of our supplier performance options available to us as one of the largest consumers of raw materials for the bedding industry in North America. I listened to all the issues we were having and hung up with the buyer to immediately search for the contract agreement in the file cabinet. Yes, at that time the cloud was only good for rain and airplane turbulence. We had our laptop hard drive that only we had access to, company servers no one outside of IT knew how to access, and good old reliable physical files. Most of the signed copies were in the physical files so it made sense to start there. Today, you can scan things from your phone directly to the cloud, right?

So, I searched the physical files and eventually stumbled upon the agreement. It appears we have every resource available to us to remove this supplier if we wanted to with nothing but a 30-day notice. However, I took pride in my ability to potentially broker this relationship between "problem supplier" and my company colleagues on the frontline who are forced to deal with the supplier every day.

The salesman was a guy named Vance. Pretty nice guy and very charismatic. A lot of our bedding lumber for the mattress foundation which we called box springs came from Canada so if you can imagine, Vance had the French-Canadian accent and sharp pronunciation to complement his denials of wrongdoing and his company's lack of performance.

However, he agreed to meet me at our manufacturing facility to discuss the issue and see if we could come to a mutual resolution. Here is where things got interesting and I learned that all deals need to be as solid as a ROCK.

The main issue was the on-time performance of Vance's shipments of lumber to our manufacturing facility in High Point, NC. The plant explained to me that the supplier shipments were hit or miss depending on the week and it made it harder to manage a production schedule and keep inventory levels low. These are common business complexities in the supply chain and not unique to this situation; however, I had to see what I could do to help us out of this jam. So, to my fault, I trusted our plant personnel and created a deal with them that if the vendor didn't get it right over the next 30 days, I would have a backup supplier ready to ship us product. Now all of us in the procurement discipline know that switching cost is more than just calculating the cost of the new supplier's product vs. the old supplier's product. However, this is what I committed to exploring and I would have to learn a ton about lumber to even begin doing this research. It's in my best interest to work with Vance to get the situation resolved.

On this journey, what I learned about moisture rates, cracks, and twist of softwood lumber still stick with me to this day. I still used that information to connect with procurement professionals across the world responsible for sourcing wood. The only difference is that some countries call it lumber and some countries call it timber.

Using the ROCK Model, I knew that if I understood the RISK TOLERANCE, considered OPERATIONAL PROCESS, calculated the COMMERCIAL IMPACT, and accounted for KNOWLEDGE TRANSFER, I would have a better chance for a solid deal.

Starting with *risk*, I knew the impact of the product and what would happen if we didn't have it on time. As far as the *operational* process, my plant colleagues supported me with this information, so I didn't see a need to question that area. I, of course, knew *commercially* at this time what the market for lumber looked like and knew that I could make a switch if needed. Lastly, most suppliers in the marketplace had enough *knowledge* about the bedding industry to quickly get ramped up and we didn't have any "tribal knowledge" ties to our current supplier, so I felt good about the knowledge transfer.

Armed with all elements of a solid ROCK I was ready for the meeting. Vance, with a couple of his colleagues, seemed to know something I didn't know as I met him in the front lobby where he patiently sat and waited for me to pick him up and escort him back to the conference room where my manufacturing team was waiting. Reading the "Preliminary Motive" of a man in which I was meeting face-to-face for the first time, I got the sense that not only was he not fearful of losing the business, but he was a facial smirk shy of acting as if we should be honored to have him as a supplier. A couple of hours later, I would understand this observation much better.

After deeper dialog with all the parties involved, it appeared my company didn't have their act together and Vance was aware of this going into the meeting.

He came equipped with documentation of all our last-minute rush orders. He even had emails from plant management thanking him for the flexibility of his company. Most impactful to our approach, he was able to demonstrate all of the on-time shipments he made in which our plant's receiving operation was not ready for his trucks and he had to incur overtime for his drivers as they sat and waited for a dock door to become available.

Vance taught me a very important lesson about why you need a plan for all four of the ROCK elements if you are going to even remotely have a chance at influencing a deal which could be as solid as a ROCK. He called me on the process as my mother had done to so many in her uncompensated tenure of influential leverage awesomesauce.

Now, let me cover the four areas of the ROCK so you don't make the same mistake I made in trying to influence Vance. However, before we jump right into four areas to master deal closure, let's agree that preparing for the negotiation, executing the negotiation and closing the deal are three unique standalone influence activities that require their unique skillsets. So, in the spirit of helping you close deals large and small, I want to share a few more techniques I've learned over the years to remember the high-level things I needed to ensure tracking and coverage of my key wants and needs. These four considerations below would apply whether negotiating with a persistent street vendor in the Dubai Souk Markets or orchestrating a complex corporate facilities negotiation for a $22 billion USD organization. I've learned that a great negotiation is only as good as what ends up on paper. To help us all avoid common deal closure mistakes, I will share four influence considerations to master so you can impress your spouse, family, or boss during negotiations.

Again, the four areas which should assist you in closing deals more successfully are Risk Consideration, Operational Process, Commercial Impact, and Knowledge Transfer.

1. Risk Consideration

The first thing you want to consider is the RISK of doing or not doing business. Four immediate concepts of doing business which should be considered with your primary option and even back up options before the negotiation begin are:

- risk of product failure
- risk of process failure
- risk of people failure
- risk of performance failure

Despite all the fancy vernacular attorneys have given us to forget the meanings of words (i.e. indemnification, limits of liability, consequential damages, etc.), we must stay focused and keep things simple. One way to keep it simple is to always remember to think with the end in mind. Know what product, process, people or performance indicators constitute success in your deal and understand the impact of anything short of those results. Once you identify and document what you need to protect in spirit, attorney friends or general council colleagues may apply the finishing touches to illustrate your point in the contract.

2. Operational Process

We all know that famous line in movies when things take a turn, right? For example when the Analyst says to the Chief of Intelligence, "You are going to want to see this." Just as your curiosity is piqued when you hear that line, so is the other side of the table when you give them intelligence of how something works or could work. With that being said, whether you are a sales leader working with a new client, a procurement leader convincing your internal stakeholders to move forward, or a first-time homebuyer influencing your spouse that living downtown won't be that loud, operational vision is PARAMOUNT! Always ensure you have a clear vision of how the next steps in the process should look, how a person will be trained or how a product will be packaged and shipped. When I negotiated $125 million USD a year of global packaging deals for a paper and packaging company, I was always curious about how they processed my order, their shipping method, how it was going to fit on our shelves, and how it was loaded on our finishing and shipping equipment. In personal life, we are all guilty of buying that TV on sale which barely fits in our car. (Hint: take it out the box but leave it in the foam!)

Overall, the Operational Process is where I failed in the deal with Vance. I left it up to my colleagues and I didn't dig deeper into what leading factors may have led to the late shipments from our side internally.

3. Commercial Impact

Is it all about the Benjamins baby?! It depends! The commercial impact of closing the deal relates to all the direct and indirect financial activities. This includes and goes well beyond just the price. Savvy negotiators are always aware of the TOTAL impact of their decisions on their family's bank account or their company's income, balance sheet, and cash flow statements. In other words, ensure you can measure:

- the bottom-line profitability,
- the value of assets
- the impact on cash

Make it a point to aim to learn just as much about the other side's financials as you may know about your own. I have learned that Best Buy employees don't get paid commission. However, if you establish a personal connection, they don't mind pointing you to the "open box" product that works just as well or the upcoming sale that you will want to wait a couple of days for. Whenever I hear "G'Sean, you are going to want to see this" in a Best Buy store from the salesperson, I know I am on to something good.

4. Knowledge Transfer

Some years ago, I was in Toronto and seemed to have the same interest in stores as one lovely couple pacing ahead of me. I noticed the man was carrying her rather large purse from store to store. I realized that he figuratively and literally got stuck with the bag! In negotiations, make sure you don't get stuck with the bag. In other words, make sure you ask the right questions in advance to avoid misunderstanding. Read the warranties, read the reviews and don't be afraid to ask direct questions which requires the other side of the table to provide operational know-how. For example:

- How does this product work?
- How is your process proven?
- How are your people trained?

For the lovely couple in Toronto, maybe the gentleman should have asked, "How is carrying a heavy purse around town after hours of shopping in those shoes going to work for you?" before leaving the house with his significant other. On second thought, that approach may have been worse than just getting stuck with the bag. He may have gotten hit with the bag!

Well, some things in life we may never resolve, but I hope these four areas provide clarity on how to make sure your deals are ROCK solid!

If ROCK is a great model for influencing the closure of a deal, then you are going to want to see the Business Case in the next chapter to get deals started.

CHAPTER 6
Show Me the Money
(Driving the Business Case)

Many people flat out struggle with the ability to influence decisions whether in personal life or at the office. For example, have you ever wondered how your little sister or brother got away with so much more than you did growing up or how your colleague Tim gets to go to all the industry conferences, and you don't? If you haven't ever wondered these things, then maybe you are "Tim" or the "little sibling." Maybe you are both in life?!

Although there are some shortcuts to influence which most people would say you need to be born with, the rest of us will need to continuously sharpen our ability to sell the business case as one of the first steps.

However, before we go down that path, many of us may talk about or hear the term "business case" often but still don't know exactly what that means. I've been formally studying and practicing Business, Procurement, and Supply Chain since 1996 and to this day I sometimes still struggle with developing business cases.

Most parents may not know what a business case is, but if they are honest, they can tell you what a business case is not. For example, have you ever run out of reasons why you didn't allow your child to do something and out of nowhere, just like your parents, said, "because I said so"? If you are not a parent, you may have even found yourself saying this as an uncle, an aunt, a bigger brother or a bigger sister. We have all been there!

This, of course, is a form of influence. However, your position of power only lasts if people respect that power. Unless strategically placed, a Posture play should be one of the last resorts of influential leadership in most cases. Although a quick and easy Dynamic of Influence, Posture plays may often lead to standoffs that may be hard to back out of. Also, unless you have a certain Personal Negotiation Style and a certain title it is hard to tell your boss you don't want greasy pizza because you just told him so.

For the business case, I have learned that keeping it simple is a good thing. Keeping it simple is oftentimes saying more. Think about this for example, there are no PowerPoint slides to review on the golf course or in the cafeteria line where you may find yourself trying to influence colleagues or friends regarding something on your mind. You can't break out a projector to show your latest Excel conclusions when you see your children or little cousins running around the house knocking stuff over. Great influencers are just as good verbally on the fly as they are in scheduled meetings with visual aids.

From my travels and experience with Fortune 500 leaders, I have learned that the best thing I could do to influence the business case of being acknowledged and promoted was to provide my immediate and higher up leadership team with value. However, sometimes it is hard to measure consistent value without the formula. So here it is! Here is the magic business case calculation and it's simpler than you may have thought. Value = Benefits/Cost. I told you it was simple. The hard part is understanding the details needed to solve for benefits and costs. With that said, let's break down this concept a little further with thoughts for both articulating benefits and understanding the total cost. However, remember the calculation is only as good as the efforts to mitigate risk associated with the path forward of any personal engagement or work project. In summary, let's go deeper to:

- Articulate Benefits
- Understand Total Cost
- Mitigate Risk

1. Articulate Benefits. First, there is nothing worse than giving your all for a project and getting to what you think is the finish line only to have your manager, leadership team, or client not understand why they should move forward with your proposal or approach. With all the possible details of any given project, sometimes we forget to simply articulate the *benefit*. So, here are simple examples to put on your checklist to gain solid trust.

Essentially, you must define the benefits to your audience in a way that resonates with them and satisfies their individual needs. On a personal level, I have seen benefits illustrated in dollars, growth, and access among other measures. Professionally, consider things like cost savings, revenue growth, market penetration, etc. Aligning on benefits applicable to your audience is one way to foster trust.

For my managers, I have always created benefit by taking things off their "to-do list" so they could focus on things they enjoyed doing more with that extra time. Secondly, I always made sure I knew the top three objectives on their mind and my work always linked to one of those objectives every chance I got to report out my status. Linking your work to theirs allows them to subliminally calculate the value of having you around.

2. Understand Total Cost. The cost of obtaining benefits shall be understood and measured in dollars. Personally, this could be itemized as time, resources, or sacrificing money out of your pocket. Professionally, the same items are articulated as things like project full-time equivalents (FTE), cost of goods, overhead, working capital impact, and opportunity cost. Knowing your numbers goes a long way to develop trust and trust is one of the easiest roads to influence.

In my quest of getting promoted, I made sure I didn't make costly mistakes which superseded the value I gained in my approach to bring benefits to my leaders. If my boss had to take my work and edit it before showing it to their boss, I made sure to reduce their "cost of conversion" the next time.

3. Mitigate Risk. Last, but not least, you want your audience to fully understand the risk of moving forward. Most successful influencers would incorporate numbers and percentages wisely. Either way, the key to risk mitigation is to identify which risks are customary vs. which risks shall be identified and neutralized with the appropriate actions. Remember, it is most likely your observation of applicable risk which will demonstrate how tuned in to the audience you are. This helps to solidify trust.

In getting promoted, I had to show my managers that there was someone ready to backfill my current role to seamlessly meet current responsibilities, in addition to me already having exposure and a jump-start on the new role I was aiming for to save onboarding time. This could be done by already knowing the stakeholders or building a friendly relationship in advance with the new team.

In Summary. Let's bring it all home with a personal life example. Let's relate the value equation to buying your first car out of college. Finally, the solid workhorse that got you through college has clunked out. Instead of the typical sedan, you are trying to influence yourself, and maybe your parents, to get the sleek new sports car. Just like the parenting approach of "I told you so", you could take the approach of "I just deserve it." However, if you are truly working on your influential leverage, practice makes perfect, right?

Rule #5: If you can't prove the value to yourself, it may be even harder proving it to someone else.

Let's start with the benefit. You will need more than just how good you look in the car. You may want to find an automobile with a history of carrying a resale value which will be higher than the balance left on your loan four years from now when you go to sell it. That's a tangible benefit you can measure.

Next is the total cost. In this case, it may be centered around the affordability of the car, both at purchase and the life cycle of maintenance and gas for a quick example.

Lastly, is risk mitigation. Prove to yourself or your parents that you will carry the right insurance coverage in the event someone runs into you or dings your door in the tight squeeze parking lot at a shopping mall while you are shopping at a KB's Toy Store or something.

If all the above is calculated and articulated well, you have created the value of buying that sports car. Whether or not that convinces you or your parents to go out and buy that sports car is not really what I was looking for. Just like mattresses, I get no commission. I more so wanted you to feel how the process works on you to better prepare you to more scientifically leverage your positive influence on someone else.

One of the things you may have observed pop up in each area of the equation is *trust*. Most leaders will tell you that trust is earned. In both personal life and professional life, trust appears to be a matter of connecting and relating with the audience. The better your structure to leverage influence, the better your chances of developing and sustaining trust. At the end of the day, people shall continuously work on their influence skills because in this world almost everything is negotiable! Is everything negotiable?

CHAPTER 7

Is Everything Negotiable?

You never want to be the one who missed out because you're the one who never asked! In my life, sometimes I've had to learn things the hard way although I often try to learn things the easy way. In one case, I realized that some things I learned the hard way ran in my family. You might say some things we learn and some things we are born with.

It was the mid-eighties and I was in the first or second grade. I remember aiming to run home as fast as I possibly could. I was the first to hit the push bar door to transition my schoolmates from the confines of our all-day classroom to Trojan Street. Just a few stairs, a 10-foot concrete landing and I am now rounding the gates going left. One street, two streets, and I'm now on my block. What is usually three blocks away to get home now seems like three miles. One block down and now only two blocks to go.

In Detroit, one city block has 15 houses on each side. At the second stop sign, I looked for cars as I shook from side to side and wiggled my legs. I'm the second house from the corner, however, I live at the end of the block. I remember this moment like it was yesterday! I got in front of Mr. Columbo's house and couldn't take it anymore. Right there down the leg of my new gray corduroy pants, I felt the warm, yet uncomfortable wet stream. There I am, the age of 7 or 8 years old accepting my defeat and there wasn't even a sheet I could hide in my dirty clothes hamper in the middle of the night. Yes, I admit it, I couldn't hold it any longer.

How did I get to this point you ask? That is a great question! Well, it may be hard to believe for most of the people who know me today, but I was quite shy as a kid. Just an hour or so before this point, I remember having to really use the restroom. Unfortunately, I had missed my "IWO" or "Influence Window of Opportunity" to convince Ms. LeBlanc of an unscheduled restroom break, especially when she most likely saw me courting my young crush. Her name was Misty. I will tell that story in a different book. I was also thinking about how I was going to have to raise my hand in front of the entire room and ask my teacher out loud to use the restroom. As a somewhat shy kid, I didn't have to speak Spanish to know this was No Bueno!

Fast forward a little over a decade from that moment. I am now a freshman in college at Michigan State University (Did I say go Green!?). I get the unfortunate call that my grandmother has passed away and my father wanted to know if I was going to make the 12-hour drive with him to Mississippi for the funeral. Of course!

As you may have experienced, with any death, family members are running all over the place to sort things out and make sure final preparations are in order. I somehow recall everyone leaving the farmhouse in that small Mississippi town my father grew up in. It gave me what seemed like hours alone with my granddad. This is one of the rare times I've had alone with him. The first time I recalled was kindergarten when my dad picked me up from school and treated me and what seemed like a much younger granddad to Burger King. With my dad taking a phone call at that time, I just sat and answered my granddad's questions and attentively listened for his next set of questions.

This time, about 11 years later as a young adult, I have so many questions about myself. Questions about my bloodline, our family, and my granddad the man. Although I focused mostly on my granddad, I would learn a valuable lesson about myself at this moment. About the third or fourth question into my full-blown "Oprah" like interview, I asked my granddad what would be one of the things he would change about himself if he could. His response was honest and a little eerie. It would help me confirm my growth and solidify my leadership journey. It would help me realize that some people accept life the way it is, and some people drive life the way they want it to be.

He shared with me that he learned a valuable lesson very early in grade school. He shared with me that he had always been very shy as a kid growing up. He was so afraid of his teacher that he was too scared to ask her if he could use the restroom. He decided that he would just brave the 3-mile journey back to his parent's house instead of making that request in front of the entire class.

Unbelievably, just like my story 70 years later, he would give in to the urge and side-to-side shaking only to feel that warm and uncomfortably wet feeling that I felt. This was possibly our little secret which my grandfather would take to his grave about five years later, or it's the best-kept secret of our family bloodline. Who knows!

Either way, I have committed my life personally and professionally to test the theory that mostly everything is indeed negotiable. More times than not in my life and career, I have realized that everything was! In hindsight, why didn't I leverage the Place

Dynamic of Influence and just ask to speak to my teacher at her desk to ask her in private if I could use the restroom? I guess trying to maneuver my legs in the perfect position to just hold it didn't allow me to think logically! Either way, I realized that I would no longer accept life as the way it is, but drive life the way I wanted it to be.

Rule #6: Almost everything in life is negotiable and other things are oftentimes worth confirming that they are not!

So, if almost everything is negotiable, how do you prepare to influence almost everything?

CHAPTER 8

Perfection Prides Preparation!

If mostly everything is negotiable, then the next question would be how much time is considered enough time to prepare for these leadership and life challenges. Remember, in negotiations, there is a *Proactive Game Plan* and *Reactive Gameplay*. Sometimes we have all the time in the world and sometimes we don't! With Proactive Game Plans, leveraging influence is often a series of calculated moves that come with many strategies and angles which should be deployed at the right time to get the best result. However, that is only one side of the coin. The other side is Reactive Gameplay where leveraging influence is a collection of quick and decisive moments when every second count and the clock is always ticking. Either way, you should respect the scenario you are in and be able to adjust your delivery accordingly. Having plenty of time to negotiate should allow for a Proactive Game Plan. On the other hand, being put on the spot invokes Reactive Gameplay. The two skill sets are not the same! I find Negotiation Gatherers typically enjoy the Proactive Game Plan more and Negotiation Hunters usually enjoy the Reactive Gameplay more.

Proactive Game Planning. First, let's address the scenario where you have plenty of time since that is a little easier for some negotiators who are a little more calculating and detail-oriented. The best approach for a Proactive Game Plan is to simulate the outcomes. Always think with the end in mind! In other words, anticipate how or where something can end and make the appropriate plans to influence that ending for yourself, your family, your friends, or your colleagues. To do this, you must ask yourself two key questions.

Question 1. What motivates the other party? This question is arguably the most important in understanding the decisions the other party makes and the future direction the other party could decide to take. One way to look at it is by treating negotiations like a newborn child. Some people say by the time you have the second child, you understand the baby is crying because they are hungry, maybe the baby couldn't make it all the way home to use the restroom, or maybe the baby is too hot or too cold among other things. Using deductive reasoning in negotiations helps you narrow down the motivation of the other party based on their situation and how the potential negotiation with you can help them into something better or out of something worse.

One way to illustrate this is via the everyday life negotiation we have all come to love! The car dealership! Most of us automatically think every salesperson is motivated to sell us a car because ultimately it's money in their pocket. We can safely assume they get a commission on every sale.

In this case, we also may assume that the higher the sales price, the higher the commission. I believed this to be 100 percent the case as well until I ran into an aggressive salesman in the Pacific Northwest a few years out of college. I wasn't actively looking for a car, but I always kept my options open whenever I saw a blowout sale with potential. I pulled into the car lot and strolled the lot knowing that someone would be chasing me down in two minutes flat. Of course, before I finished that thought, there was Chad, maybe 60 seconds or so behind. Chad caught me at a used red Camaro that was the prettiest thing on the lot that day. It was priced at about $18,000 USD or so from what I can remember. As I recall, the Kelly Blue Book was about $17,000 and some change. I remember thinking that I should "low ball" or throw out a number with little chance of getting accepted just to see how Chad would respond. I didn't need a new car anyway. However, Chad seemed like a nice guy. I remember he asked me, "Is this the type of car you could see yourself in?" Now Chad already seemed like a typical sales guy! "Of course!" was my only response. I explained to him that the price tag was close to being in line with KBB and I didn't want to spend that much on a car. I also let him know I was just looking. Then Chad said something I was not expecting to hear. It was against all my beliefs about salespeople and commission. He said to me, "I am sure I can come closer to whatever price you give me than you have to come to mine." Now I am intrigued as to what is motivating Chad. However, I want to test his position first. I recall tossing out the number of $12k and told him that's about where I wanted to be with monthly payments. I knew that every $1,000 equaled about $18/month in payments. Seeming impressed with my financial preparation, Chad said, "I am sure we can make a deal." After going back and forth for a little while, Chad comes back with a number of $14.8k or $14.9k. I remember thinking that he did come closer to me than I came to him. Wow!

I never ended up buying that Camaro. However, I know I would have looked amazing in that car. One of my best friends at the time, Lisa, convinced me that it is not the most practical car for the family man I was going to be. That made sense to me then, however, 17 years later I still did not need to squeeze car seats in the back of the car yet. Oh well!

It turned out that another good friend of mine, Tony, knew Chad as well. He was in the process of buying an Acura from Chad a few months later. Rolling with Tony during one of his trips to the dealership, I had an opportunity to ask Chad what motivated him to reduce the price of that Camaro a few months back. He recalled our quick negotiation and told me that the challenge that month for the sales team was to get as many cars off the lot as they could to get ready for the new models coming in. He said that the bonus for selling cars was $500 and the only rule was to sell the used cars for $1 above the dealer's trade-in.

I was reminded that knowing someone's motivation is extremely key to influential leverage. In the case with the Camaro, both Chad and I had separate motivations which could have resulted in a mutually beneficial deal for both of us. That was good to learn!

Question 2. When do you know a deal is right? How many of us are guilty of shopping all day only to conclude that the first item we saw was "The One"? This happens all the time, both in personal life and as a professional negotiator. In my line of business, it's easy to travel the world for the best supplier and realize that the best option is the next state over. Another example is how we look at universities all over the country for us or our children and end up picking the one right next to home. In either situation, a key to knowing if the deal is right is to manage and measure your parameters. Parameters are the items in which you are comfortable accepting in the event acceptable ranges of those items are met during a negotiation. You have two approaches to parameter range acceptance when it comes to leverage.

The first approach which I call a Singular Clause Negotiation would be to see each parameter as its separate discussion and to focus on one parameter at a time. An example would be me negotiating a bistro table set at a Home and Garden store. I would focus on the price first to find an acceptable price for what I am trying to pay. After the price is agreed on, I would then see the best turnaround time I can get the pieces delivered to my house.

The second approach which I call a Dynamic Clause Negotiation would be to only conclude with acceptance of a certain parameter, if and only if, a minimum of one other parameter is also in line with your needs. Using the same bistro table set example, I would negotiate a certain price range. I would only accept that price if they also agreed that they can deliver the items to my house which is 15 miles away by tomorrow afternoon.

Either approach is acceptable depending on the complexity of the deal you are trying to make and the negotiation style of the person you find yourself negotiating with.

Nevertheless, regardless of the negotiation parameters set, you still need to know when that singular or dynamic negotiation is the right approach for you. The best way to do this is to understand your needs. Most deals have three different needs. Those three needs are Commercial, Operational, and Legal.

Commercial. You want to make sure the deal financially fits your pocketbook. In this space, it is important to know what you can afford, what is the total cost, and how the cash flows. In other words, you want to have your arms around the budget regarding what you can and can't afford. Corporations and small businesses measure this by their Profit & Loss Statement, otherwise known as the Income Statement. You will want to ensure no hidden costs in completely understanding the total cost. Our industry calls this understanding the TCO's or total cost of ownership. It is knowing the total cost of oil changes, maintenance, and insurance on that Camaro in addition to the purchase price. Lastly, you will want to know how and when money exchanges hands to control cash flow. Corporations and small businesses have the Cash Flow Statement to dictate when the transaction could happen and the Balance Sheet to understand the impact of the transaction.

Operational. You want to focus on the process map of how things would work. For example, how to take possession of the bistro set, how to redeem the warranty, and does the delivery usually includes setting up or disposal of old furniture, etc.

Legal. It's typically stuff we leave up to our attorney friends or general council at our job. However, the summary is any need that will be considered to reduce the risk and liability of that transaction. In the example of the bistro table, we want to ensure it does have some type of manufacturer's warranty. We may even be curious as to what happens if the company goes out of business.

In summary, there are two key questions you have to ask yourself in a proactive game plan scenario: *"How do you motivate the other party?"* and *"When do you know a deal is right?"*

Reactive Gameplay. Now let's look at the Reactive Gameplay scenario where you have limited time to respond. A great example would be face-to-face or across the table from the other party working through a Singular or Dynamic Clause Negotiation. In this situation, we used the word gameplay instead of game plan on purpose. You may have to be ready to go back and forth with the other party. Here, the same questions which were important for the Proactive Game Plan apply. Also, we must add two more questions when we talk about preparing for Reactive Game Play.

The first additional question is: How do they benefit from the position they are taking or the statement they just made? A lot of people are guilty of quickly responding with an emotional yes or no to questions without logically understanding how the other party benefits from the answer to the question. When some people answer too quickly, they are guilty of "giving away the farm." In other words, they often disclose information and share their strategies without getting anything in return. Again, depending on the Negotiation Style discussed in Chapter 3 and the Leverage Philosophy discussed in Chapter 10 of who you are dealing with, this could be the start to a good trusting relationship or a disaster for your company or family waiting to happen.

The second question is: How do you want the situation to end? Most negotiators who are comfortable with confrontation understand that most influential moments come by default with a range of emotions. Of course, negotiations for any given party could result in temporary anger, sadness, spite, defeat, or hopelessness at any given moment. If you are the party who has inflicted the pain on the other party, you have to understand what damage control is necessary to ensure you don't permanently lose their attention or give them a reason to want to retaliate.

For example, when I find myself tricked into watching *"Real Housewives"* with my significant other, I realize the ladies who control leverage are those who are most comfortable with confrontation. However, that fearless confrontation must be balanced by that person's ability to have an Influential Postmortem. What is the Influential Postmortem? It's the moment or moments after the blowout when they corner the other party, usually one-on-one. They usually cry together, literally and figuratively, about why the truth had to be spoken and how they did and said things during the climax because they care about each other's wellbeing. It doesn't happen exactly that way in real business to business negotiations between multi-billion-dollar companies, but I wanted to prove examples of influence could be pulled from anywhere.

All in all, preparing for negotiations is about knowing what questions to strategically ask yourself and the other party. Remember the "other party" could often be someone on your team.

Rule #7: Most Negotiation Gatherers Proactively Game Plan well and most Negotiation Hunters have great Reactive Gameplay, but great influencers understand, respect, and execute both!

For great influencers to do both, it is often important to have a formal or informal team of support. Whether a boss or team member who is interested in joining you for a deal discussion or a significant other and friend that you drag along with you to look at a house, make sure everyone is clear on their influence roles.

CHAPTER 9

Negotiating with the Crew (Mastering Team Dynamics)

Whether trying to figure out the details of your new job offer or buying that new car, most times it's easier to have a team supporting us, right? These players are formal and informal resources who help us navigate complex situations, explore alternative options, question "Preliminary Motives", and/or confirm we are landing a good deal. In life, we are usually the person who *takes* a friend or loved one to the car dealership or the friend or loved one that is *asked* to tag along to the dealership, right? For most people - not all-there is something about having a negotiation crew that feels right! I agree that it's usually never a good idea to negotiate by yourself when you have the option available to have friends or colleagues witness discussions and possibly, at minimum, help you recall and piece together the nature of discussions afterward. In rare situations, this team approach could have negative consequences if not managed carefully.

For example, in 2005, I was negotiating a deal for $10 million USD or so with a few suppliers. One thing each one of these suppliers had in common was the supplier that they all used for the substrate. The substrate was one of the base materials they used as a raw material for the product produced for my company. Knowing that the substrate was critical to the success of their product, we secretly brought in the tier II supplier who was all of our pending suppliers' supplier, to ask them a few questions about their product and how they saw it being used to give us the best outcome. The discussion consisted of four people from their leadership team and five people from our internal cross-functional group. We had representation from Research & Development,

Operations, and Engineering. I am representing the Global Procurement group.

During this conversation, the supplier decided to have an open dialog with us about not only their product but the utilization of each of their customers who happened to be in the group of suppliers we were planning to negotiate with. I thought was a bold move by a tier II supplier, but I had to understand their Preliminary Motive. As I thought through the scenario, this supplier was going to get the business either way as they were a supplier for all three suppliers on our radar.

Considering this new open and honest dialog, one of the areas that we felt important for us to cover was their thoughts on their customer's quality and the ability to use their materials the right way to get to our finished product. I directly asked them to share their feedback on each of the three options we had on our list. Leaning towards one option over the others, we were quite intrigued by what they had to say about this particular supplier to us and customer to them. To our disbelief, they shared with us that this option's end product wasn't the best because of their inability to blend their substrate enough to be evenly spread across the finished good. They went on to give us details about their manufacturing process and the pros and cons. The conversation ended with our Research & Development leader asking them if they happened to have any product samples in which they could show us the lack of uniformity of our first supplier option. The company agreed to send those samples over and I, of course, didn't think much of it since that level of detail was more operational in nature. However, I committed to the company that these discussions were confidential, and we appreciated their transparency.

A few weeks later, I decided to engage the same internal cross-functional team to have commercial negotiations with the three suppliers. The first up was our first pick option with the potential quality issues disclosed by their raw material supplier. The discussions are going well, and it seems like we are getting traction until the discussion shifted to product quality.

Of course, we pressed them on their ability to evenly spread their raw materials throughout their final product and whether this would present a problem for them in the future if we awarded them the business. After repeatedly allowing them to save face and be open and transparent with us things took a turn. Our Research & Development leader pulled out a bag from under the table. Ed said, "I hear what you are telling us but inside of this bag we have samples in which we have ran testing of your materials and you can see the inconsistencies." This was a typical scope, specification, and quality discussion except for one huge delivery issue.

The bag in which he pulled out for his grand negotiation zinger had the logo and branding of their supplier all over it. He never transferred the samples from their bag to our company bag. Maybe even any bag without their raw material supplier's name on it for that matter. Yes, the company that openly shared all the transparent information and we promised extreme confidentiality, 100 percent exposed!

After playing damage control for the next 30-60 days or so, I had time to reflect on what I possibly did wrong. At first, I thought it may have been a good idea in hindsight if I decided to negotiate with the supplier without involving my internal stakeholders. This seemed like a logical solution going forward, but I also know that there had to be something I could have done differently while still reaping the benefit of having a crew engaged.

After talking with others in the industry, I concluded that I set myself up for failure from the start. Although having a team supporting you during negotiations is a good thing, I never aligned with the team on roles and responsibilities. Since that point, I have always defined at least four default roles when it comes to team negotiations.

The first role I've identified as necessary is the Facilitator. The Facilitator is the person who sets and communicates the logistics and agenda of the negotiation. They align schedules and find the ideal environment for the negotiations to take place. This person is usually organized, takes good notes, and has very good communication during Proactive Game Planning.

The second role identified is the Lead Negotiator. The Lead Negotiator is ultimately the person who defines and communicates the overall strategy. They continuously evaluate the needs and whether they are close to getting what they are looking for. They usually decide whether to deploy Singular Clause Negotiations or Dynamic Clause Negotiations and are usually pretty sharp with Reactive Gameplay.

The third role is the Subject Matter Expert. The Subject Matter Expert (or the SME) is the person who may take a deeper dive into identified subject matters like machine operations, environmental law, etc. This person is usually highly knowledgeable on a subject, has years of experience, or has gone through a similar process or engagement before in the area in which they are providing expertise. This person is like a best friend who worked at a company you are interviewing with.

Lastly, to round out the team is the Research & Analytics Leader. The Research & Analytics Leader, like the SME, can speak to many areas with a level of expertise. However, this expertise usually comes from quick, pointed research performed specifically for the negotiations at hand. This person is usually good at gathering data and takes pride in the presentation of the use of that data.

So again, we have the Facilitator, the Lead Negotiator, the SME, and the Research & Analytics Leader.

Unfortunately, many of us don't have ample resources in our negotiations and are forced to play many roles. In this case, I would suggest ensuring that you are appropriately representing the key roles and responsibilities of each role.

When I was in the Home Furnishing industry, I was forced to negotiate some of our smaller $5 million USD deals by myself because the negotiations were more informal and happened throughout conferences, telephone calls, golfing rounds, and often while driving to and from work. In these cases, I made it a point to ensure I incorporated the key essentials of each role.

For example, as the Facilitator, I always defined the best time for me to partake in negotiations versus moments where I just wanted to gather data.

Rule #8: Never allow anyone to decide when you are ready until you are truly ready.

I realized it was ok for me to tell someone I was going to call them back when I got to my desk. I didn't want to start trying to recall numbers off the top of my head unless I felt extremely comfortable that I knew enough to do it successfully.

As the Lead Negotiator, I always had a good grasp over all the key parameters, facts, and opinions associated with any negotiation. Again, this goes back to having a balance of all integrated commercial, operational, and legal elements of a deal. I knew when I could speak to a subject intelligently or when I should engage a Subject Matter Expert or Research & Analytics Leader.

As a Subject Matter Expert, I typically always knew what parameters I could explain from experience. This usually includes how to do business with my company, what commercial terms are acceptable to review, which were not, and what the marketplace competition looked like, among many other areas of subject expertise.

Lastly, when it comes to Research & Analytics leadership, I focused on the demographics regarding the company or the other party I was dealing with. I also focused on my cost modeling and understanding what others were paying for <u>M</u>aterials, <u>L</u>abor, <u>O</u>verhead, and Acceptable <u>P</u>rofits.

Rule #9: Know Your MLOP like your ABC's.

I learned that not knowing your numbers is basically like negotiating walking through your house in the dark. You could get it right by chance but now and then you will sacrifice a head, shoulder, knee or toe.

Nevertheless, whether leading a team or working independently, it is important to set and agree on the responsibilities of each role to ensure you are not missing key activities needed to allow your ability to influence outcomes to thrive.

In our personal lives, these roles are just as significant. Let's take the example of dating. The Facilitator in you will define when you meet up with someone and how much time you spend with them. The Lead Negotiator will find direct and creative ways to see if they are serious without showing your cards. The Subject Matter Expert would impress them with your knowledge of museums, cooking, rock climbing, or whatever you consume your time with outside work. Lastly, the Research & Analytics Leader in you stalks their social media to try to find out if they are the person they say they are. If you are too busy to be the Research & Analytics Leader, most people usually have that one friend, parent, or family member who has no problem volunteering to take that role behind the scenes or even grill them face to face. I call them Negotiation Pit Bulls! It's always good to have a Pit Bull on your side of the fence!

CHAPTER 10

Balancing Leverage Philosophies

Whether with a team or rolling solo, you must get ready to adjust and adapt to the type of negotiation or dynamics of leverage activity you are involved in. Often your negotiation style will influence your expectations of others' negotiation styles. For example, if you are easy-going, you may prefer to work with easy-going people. If you are direct and to the point, you may prefer to work with people who are direct and to the point. There is nothing wrong with having this preference when engaging in negotiations. The issue is more so when you assume that people are wired the way you are wired. This is called *"Mirror*

Image Fallacy" and was introduced by Dr. Charles Krauthammer in his best-seller "Things That Matter."

One way to quickly illustrate this concept is in the dating circle. If you are open and transparent, then you tend to want to deal with people who are open and transparent. Again, there is nothing wrong with this approach. However, it could be a disaster to assume that everyone you meet and grow fond of will be open and transparent. When you engage someone who is, it may work out just fine. However, when you assume someone is and it turns out that they are more guarded and secretive, is usually when the leverage mismatch occurs. So just how you should avoid this fallacy in a personal relationship, you should avoid this pitfall in negotiations and influence.

To help avoid this mismatch of leverage, we must understand Leverage Philosophies. Leverage Philosophies are those relationship approach expectations you operate by and may assume others to operate by. Three common types that I have seen in my career are the Collaboration Partnership, Competitive Winner, and the Forced Union.

The *Collaborative Partnership* is usually a dynamic where all sides of the negotiation have a vested interest to openly participate and find mutually beneficial results for all parties. Your negotiation partner or partners are often open to strategizing on what is best for all parties and willing to take a critical look at processes and policies which may need to be changed to break through perceived roadblocks.

I find myself in these types of negotiations often and enjoy the fact that you don't have to consistently watch your back all the time. All of us will find ourselves vulnerable from time to time and having a partner who identifies this vulnerability and what it means to the joint team instead of exploiting it is very comforting. You may share subject matter experts if the trust is mutual and the lead negotiators are usually focused on mutual beneficial growth.

The *Competitive Winner* aims to win mostly at all costs and creates an environment where all sides of the negotiation must carefully ensure that their vested interests are addressed and there are minimum loopholes in their agreements. Your negotiation partner or partners are usually open to debate on topics based on the level of importance to them. You must ensure not to address too many of their parameters without ensuring balance from your end.

I also find myself in these types of negotiations from time to time and enjoy the fact that you are forced to stay competitive and on your toes. You must ensure you understand all angles of the discussion and engage subject matter experts in areas where you don't. Lead Negotiators are usually focused on self-beneficial growth by default and mutual growth where they can ensure their embedded victory in that growth.

Lastly, *Forced Union* is usually a relationship where all sides of the negotiation thrive to make the best out of a situation where they must participate either due to the situation or to satisfy a third party's needs. The other party often interested in sticking to the pre-defined rules of engagement or doing the minimum required to ensure their basic needs are always satisfied. An example would be a loyal customer who forces you to work with a mandated supplier or a double date in which you immediately know is going nowhere but dinner is at your favorite restaurant!

All good negotiators need to identify the type of Leverage Philosophy you feel is appropriate for the type of relationship and influence applicable. *"Mirror-Image Fallacy"* could be devastating in this situation so take the time to truly see and understand the other party's intentions. If you go into the relationship under the Collaborative Partner premise and the other party is in a Competitive Winner mindset, you may find yourself giving away the farm again. If you go in with a Competitive Winner and the other party has a more Collaborative Partner approach, you may turn the other party off from future collaborations. If you go in assuming a Forced Relationship because of a third-party introduction and the other party has more of a collaborative partnership mindset, you may come off as being in it for yourself and ruin a promising new relationship.

Rule #10: The person who understands Leverage Philosophies singularly can dominate a discussion from time to time, however, the person who applies Leverage Philosophies dynamically controls the relationship most of the time.

Just because you start a relationship under the premise of one Leverage Philosophy doesn't mean you always have to end there. A lot of good friends I have today and collaborate with often where introduce through third parties. In some cases, neither one of us kept in contact with that third-party. Also, some people which I've butted heads with originally have become great resources in my life.

Either way, just as much as you shall pay attention to Leverage Philosophies, you should pay attention to techniques.

CHAPTER 11

Don't Sweat Their Technique

I've always felt the most sustainable influence technique is an open dialog backed by trust and the appropriate amount of transparency. Unfortunately, sometimes trust or transparency is not reciprocated immediately by the other party. When you find yourself in this situation, verbal and nonverbal Influence Techniques become even more critical for influential leverage and successful outcomes.

The first person that comes to mind often for me is Mr. McCoy. At Henry Ford High School in Detroit, I finished my senior year as the Class President. My Faculty Advisor was Mr. McCoy. As a young adult, there were moments in which most of us demonstrated leadership and maturity. On the other hand, we all also had moments where our lack of judgment showed our age and inexperience. Although rare, I had "lack of judgment" moments. What I found to be interesting is Mr. McCoy always had verbal and non-verbal ways of influencing me. He always found a smooth method to leverage my desire to be great as a way of keeping things in focus for the greater good of the senior class. Mr. McCoy continuously used his dynamics of leverage on me to help shape a great senior year and a better G'Sean.

I recall one time I decided to eat cheese crackers he had leftover in his office from a field trip. I ate so many of those things I decided I didn't even need to eat lunch. He loosely suggested I stop eating so many packs of crackers, but of course, he never leveraged Posture. He knew that Prototype was more effective for my young and impressionable mind. The next day he asked me, "How was your night." I told him, "It was, ok but my stomach was killing me." It was then that he asked me the perfectly timed question, "Do you want more of these crackers today or do you think a real lunch is a better idea?"

Mr. McCoy was a master at balancing the Six Dynamics of Influence within his Influence Techniques. Sometimes he would take a direct approach and sometimes he would take an open approach. So, let's define Direct Leverage and Open Leverage before we further explore some cool Influence Techniques.

Direct Leverage - a power played or threatened to be played to force compliance or dictated alignment.

Open Leverage - a value positioned to be traded for something deemed as possibly more valuable than the original holding.

Direct Leverage directly applies pressure like, "I have another job offer unless you give me that director-level role that's open." Open Leverage openly accepts options like, "I have another job offer but I'd rather stay here if you can make something happen at the director level." Depending on the situation, it's good to have the ability to practice and deploy both types of leverage for the ultimate influence technique balance.

With awareness and understanding of Direct and Open Leverage, we will now look at Influence Techniques which could all apply Direct or Open Leverage. Although there are easily hundreds of core Influence Techniques, I will focus on a collection of techniques we have observed as more commonly leveraged and successful during our global Influential Leverage study. This includes techniques like Open Mic, Pawn Punt, Level Up, Ear Torching, Radical Repeat, Stone-Face, Busy-Bee, and Chain of Condition.

"Open Mic." Many times, people ask me if they should be the first person to take a position or if they should allow the other party to state their position. The simple answer is that it depends on the weight of leverage at that moment. If you perceive that you have leverage and the ability to bounce around from topic to topic well with dynamic grace, then you may use the "Open Mic" more often. One way to do this is by simply flat out asking the other party to explain their approach, proposal, service offering, or reason for wanting to get your attention - whichever one applies to your situation of course. The essence of this technique is your desire to understand their position and possibly getting them to alter it while you reserve the right to share yours as needed. So, you may start with a question like, "Why don't you explain more of your proposal." However, be careful because some savvy negotiators will fire back with a qualifying question like, "What do you understand so far?" In this case, you may feel like you don't want to go back and forth, and you end up giving in to the reverse "Open Mic." However, you can always respond to their reverse tactic by stating, "I certainly don't want to put words in your mouth" or "I wouldn't do you any justice summarizing your point-of-view." In summary, try to listen more than you speak to gain valuable insight. If the other party starts negotiating with themselves, you have mastered it. On the other hand, don't allow people to have you negotiating with yourself. I see this often in entrepreneurship when leaders start lowering their prices just because the customer asked what all was included.

"Pawn Punt." Ever been in a situation where you didn't want to ask or maybe didn't even know how to approach someone with a sincere inquiry? We all have been there! If you are dying to ask a question but may feel the question is a little beyond the established comfort zone with the other party, many people are good for using this technique. For example, if you are curious about hiring practices but don't want to be known as the controversial person who brought the question up, you may say, "A lot of people in my group have been asking me why our company never seems to promote from within." Again, this is a great way to punt the origin of this question to imaginary or undefined colleagues. If you find yourself on the receiving end of this type of question, you may use the phrase "that's above my paygrade" which is one of the most common avoidance methods I have seen in the industry. You are saying I don't know, and I am not even paid enough to answer that question if I tried. Just be careful because the other party could respond by asking you, "Well, who do you think would know?" The 45th President of the United States (POTUS) is great at "Pawn Punting." He will tell you something extremely flattering about himself or his presidency and follow it up with something like, "That's what people are saying!"

"Level Up." This move is often added to the back of an "Open Mic". Whether an "Open Mic" is present or not, you are attempting to take a stated position from the other party, to upgrade it in any increment which is more beneficial to you. For example, I took a cruise some years back and Mazatlán was one of our port stops. I felt it was a great time to buy some souvenirs for the family. When you have 11 nieces and nephews, you leverage influence or go broke. In this situation, I knew I was interested in buying at least two of these handmade whistles upfront. However, I didn't share this immediately. I leveraged the "Open Mic" and asked the young lady selling souvenirs to give me her best deal on <u>one</u> of these green porcelain turtle whistles. With a displayed price of $5 each, (technically the list price), she said she was able to come down to $4. I then suggested that I would be willing to buy two for $6. She asked me how about three for $10. I, of course, said, "deal." In the end, I got three for $10 instead of the original two for $10 I was already committed to buying. From her perspective selling more units and getting more revenue were her priorities.

The "Level Up" can also be reversed with a "Level Down." In the case of the whistle, when I suggested two for $6, she could have said, "I can do 3 for $10, however, one of them has a small crack you can barely see on the bottom that I was going to keep it for myself." That didn't happen, but this is a good tactic when you may want to give away something worthless to you but possibly valuable to someone else. So, keep those not so perfect items around when you are negotiating with bargain hunters.

"Ear Torch." The "Ear Torch" is more analytical than some of my Negotiation Hunters may like but it works well when you have someone who is asking too many questions. Let's take a boss who has been hands-off for the most part and all a sudden, desires to be briefed on everything you have going on. As long as you are pretty clear on their background, you can start "Ear Torching" them with so many details about the requested topic that they eventually conclude it's too much to understand and you seem to have it under control. However, be careful! You don't want that person to dislike dealing with you or feel like you always have long-winded answers every time they need quick information. Use the technique wisely and sparingly! I see this most often used by mechanics. When my mother calls me and asks me to speak to the mechanic directly, I know there is a good chance she just got "Ear Torched" by that mechanic on purpose. I am sure the mechanic tells everyone who will listen that ceramic brake pads are the only pads that will allow her to stop the car in anything over 75-degree weather because of its high heat properties and the weight of her car. With a little briefing from my mother and a quick Google search, I usually start the conversation by asking, "What is the difference of the maximum melting point of each type of brake pad option?" That type of response is usually just enough to get an "Ear Torcher" to keep it simple by saying, "We have an optional ceramic upgrade I mentioned to your mother, but the standard will work just as well since it doesn't get that warm in Virginia." However, be careful with "Ear Torching" or "Reverse Ear Torching" because someone may get excited that you understand and want to converse on a deeper technical level in which Google can't help you anymore.

"Radical Repeat." Have you ever seen a few ads for something on TV and suddenly decided that maybe you are in the mood for it? This is the power of repetition in marketing and branding. Some sales folks feel like if they repeat their value enough that eventually, the buyer will give in. Well, there is some truth to this, and it works on offense and defense. I was renting a car not too long ago and as I walked up to the board, I didn't see my name. A gentleman was sitting in front of the board with a clipboard of names. I asked him if he had Williams on the list and he said, "Yes, you can grab anything from that aisle." I then preceded to the area and picked out a car in the aisle which had my standard upgrade selection and a second level upgrade selection as well. With the instructions of "that" aisle being vague, I took him up on this direction and picked a second level upgrade. When I got to the gate, the gentlemen asked me my name and after a couple of minutes suggested that the car I picked, a special edition Ford Mustang with tons of horsepower, was only available for an extra $25 USD/per day. I was already running a little too close on time for the first meeting we flew to Houston for, so I knew I wasn't going back to pick another car. Besides, the thought of paying an extra $25 USD/per day wasn't getting me excited and I knew it would drive my father crazy. So, I went with the "Radical Repeat" approach because I don't use it that often and I wanted to see how it would work. My response was, "Unfortunately the gentlemen at the car assignment board told me to pick any car from this aisle and that is what I did." Not knowing how to respond to this, the gate agent apologized for the potential inconvenience of picking another car. However, he wasn't giving up his position and I wasn't going to give up my position either because, for every minute which ticked away on the clock, another car pulled in behind me. With moments ticking and cars waiting, one of us had to decide to get over it. Under pressure, the gate agent got on this radio to explain the situation to his manager. No longer than two minutes later, his manager came over and explained the same dilemma regarding going back and picking another car. I simply repeated the same thing I told the gate agent, however, this time and each time, I did so with a little more blatant display of respectful irritation stemming from the inconvenience. I used the opportunity to repeat my value to the gate agent and manager reminding them of how many rental cars I have rented as a "Gold Member" in the last 20 years. Also, to keep the relationship intact, I repeatedly blamed the error on their process like my mother would do to help them use it as an excuse as well. Eventually, the manager entered his override code and apologized for the error in their process. That could have gone either way, but it worked in my favor. I spent the entire trip seeing just how fast that car could go from 0 to 60mph on the highway.

Of course, we have all seen this tactic work in airports. Typically, I see foreigners in a new country use this method as a go-to. In my travels, I often hear ticket counter agents or gate agents at the airport explaining to foreigners some obscure policy or regulation. Many times, I stop and listen because there is a good chance I know where the conversation is going. With the right timing and respect, the foreigner usually says, "I don't understand." Classic! Now the airport employee is forced to repeatedly state this policy that they don't even really believe in. The success measure is hit or miss, but if you have no other approach to sneak that slightly bigger than accepted carry-on aboard the aircraft in a new country, it is worth a try.

"Stone-Face." This tactic is only possible with extreme comfort with silence and eye contact. The "Stone-Face" is an emotionless blank stare or gaze as a response to someone's inquiry or comment to you. Unfortunately, I find myself using this one often when

I continuously defy the time when taking domestic flights. To squeeze all the juice out of face to face meetings, I have been known to leave for the airport just a few minutes too late for most people's comfort. Although I am sweating bullets to the airport, in the car rental check-in line, and on the shuttle bus, I need to stay cool and calm at the ticket agent desk. If I arrive 45 minutes before the flight at a standard size airport with minimal to no security lines backed up, it usually works like a charm. With a little bit of displayed pep in my step, I calmly say I am checking in for the 3:30 pm flight to wherever and the ticket counter agent immediately looks at their watch. They typically say something like, "You think you are going to make this flight?" My response is no response. I am "Stone-Face." In doing this, I have realized that three seconds is a long-time when you are looking someone in the eyes and no words are exchanged. Most people typically can't manage silence very well for three seconds. Attacking a defenseless object is typically not an easy trait for most people either. Most times, three seconds is enough time for the ticket agent to feel bad for their first suggestion and start to give you hope. The words of hope are usually, "if you don't have any bags to check and you run, you may be able to make it."

Something about the "Stone-Face" for three seconds or more will get the other party to end up talking more. However, be careful! If the other party is a Dedicated or Extreme Negotiation Hunter, you may not like what they end up saying.

"Busy-Bee." The "Busy-Bee" tactic is strategically leveraging the clock to slow down and speed up the current discussion to your liking to throw off the rhythm of the other party. For example, we all work with people who are easily distracted by their laptops or phones when we are talking to them. This could be their nature, but it just as well could be their way of giving you a subliminal message that they will control the pace of this discussion. Do you recall the last time you ask someone for a moment of their time, and they say yes? They then looked at their watch or phone to check the current time? The immediate feeling most people would feel is that you must make sure to respect their time. Really good negotiators will use this dynamic and third parties to speed up a conversation or slow-down a conversation. For example, if I don't know where a conversation is going and I feel I may not be prepared, I always ensure the other party knows I am waiting on a call, have someone waiting on me or need to be somewhere. Therefore, if the discussion is not favorable, I remind them of my previous commitment and ask if we can pick back up the discussion later. I then use that time to ensure they don't catch me off guard a second time. On the other hand, if the discussion is favorable, I let them know that I will call the other person right-back or the person waiting on me isn't in a hurry.

If you find yourself in a live discussion going one topic at a time, you can use the "Busy-Bee" on the fly. For example, let's say you are pitching a new product to a prospective client, and you are starting negotiations. You "Open Mic" to get them to share their overall thoughts and force them to identify a list of topics they wish to cover. You can then suggest to them that you have to take a small break to check in on the office or family but suggest that you can cover the items which you feel pretty strong about really quickly first to knock them out.

Setting the tone for time allows you some level of control in situations that you may not even have any actual leverage. If you find yourself being on the other side of this negotiation tactic, get the other party to commit to how much time they have and ensure its enough for you to negotiate your points. If they try to rearrange your agenda, tell them to go ahead and make their call to check in on family now or do it at the lunch break. However, Dedicated and Extreme Negotiator Gatherers shall make sure you are comfortable with confrontation before doing that with a Dedicated or Extreme Negotiation Hunter!

"Chain of Condition." Lastly, for this book, this one is a tactic to delay and defer any important negotiation inquiry from the other party. Sometimes you don't wish to share a lot of information before making a final decision which is most favorable for you. However, while not sharing much information, you want to narrow down your options based on the best value. We see this all the time in our negotiation simulations. Most procurement professionals will do this with suppliers often as well.

For example, when I was sourcing $100 million USD worth of packaging materials, I would often encounter new suppliers. I would simply ask the supplier a collection of questions about their price, quality, specifications, capacity, etc. Then, when they return a question or two, I made everything dependent on something else. For example, when they asked me what price point they needed to be, I would say it depended on the quality of the product. When they asked me what type of quality we were looking for, I told them it depended on the site I could see them delivering to and what that site is using today. When they asked me what sites I could see them supplying, I told them it depended on their price point and how much money they could potentially save us.

This process could go on and on until you slowly retrieve enough information from the other party to make the best decision about the path forward for your needs without them truly understanding much about yours.

However, please note that this tactic takes a lot of confidence and tough skin. Essentially, continuously delaying the sharing of any solid information could be viewed as indecisive or non-collaborative. A lot of corporate supplier diversity leaders are said to be guilty of this. Our parents are repeat offenders as well.

Think about that time you first started driving and you asked one of your parents to drive their car. Most likely, the immediate response was, "Where are you trying to go?" You give them an answer, then the next question is "Who you are going with?" You give them an answer and then the next question is, "When are you trying to go?" You finally corner them with all the details and then they say, "I think your dad may need the car tonight or I may need to run to the store." You tell them you can stop by the store and suddenly, they are not sure exactly what they need from the store. Regardless of the details, our parents were great at chaining conditions on our every request. By the time you got the car, you had to take your little sibling with you and bring food back for the entire family!

CHAPTER 12

Influential Leverage for Lunch

Influence Techniques often make the difference between good strategic influence and poorly executed waste of power and leverage. It often sets extraordinary negotiators apart from average ones. Negotiations are not the same as a debate. I often define negotiations as, *the art and science of bringing parties to an alignment good enough to be documented in a contract or philosophical agreement.* I find most people who don't like negotiations, typically don't like to debate. However, a debate is more about philosophical positions which usually never come to any decisive conclusion. From what you may see on television, some attorneys debate in courtrooms for hours in front of the judge. They go back and forth sticking to a point, shifting points, and trying to prove points based on law and precedence. This to me is more of an open debate than a negotiation. However, at recess in the hallways, you can see attorneys truly negotiating on behalf of their clients. This is when deals are made, and influential leverage is at its best. So, if you don't like debates, but you like to strike a deal from time to time, negotiations might not be so bad after all.

Rule #11: Not all of us negotiate and influence outcomes for a living, however, all of us should negotiate and influence outcomes for a better quality of life.

Love the power of influence or not, having some structure and a few techniques up your sleeve may not be a bad idea.

For me, I started by learning how to negotiate life. Then it was about negotiating for leadership. Now, I find myself often negotiating for lunch.

Growing up on the streets of Detroit wasn't the safest upbringing I could have had in my life. I even grew up on the westside which was only moderately bad. My cousins grew up on the eastside and had it even worse. Westside or eastside, relatively speaking, both were tough compared to most other parts of the country.

I learned some valuable lessons on the streets of Detroit which my kids will never have to experience. I grew up in the eighties and nineties. That period was known for some cool things, but it was also known for HIV and drugs. In our neighborhood, it was crack cocaine. Luckily, not too many children in the world experience a crack cocaine epidemic just walking up and down their block every day to and from school. Also, very few people outside of a warzone can say they have seen people being shot or stabbed.

Once, at the age of 9 or 10, I sat on my uncle's porch and watched a man run from around the corner and get shot from a guy running behind him. I then saw the man bleed to death on the curb right across the street. I remember feeling sorrow and sadness. No one deserves to end their life on the curb. I wondered if he could have negotiated life better.

In Detroit, we had to negotiate life every day just to keep your valuables. The rule of thumb in the inner city was to protect yourself and then protect your belongings. Everything was fair game for possibly being jacked back then, and even still today. Jacked means getting something you own stolen from you with force or the threat of force. Being jacked makes petty theft and muggings seem more like gestures of donations when compared. In Detroit, it was a 50/50 chance that someone was going to hurt you even after you gave them your jacket, shoes, hat, chain, watch, wallet, etc.

In the seventh grade, I remember playing basketball with friends in Lamar's backyard after school about two miles away from my house. I had just convinced my sister to let me wear her leather jacket.

It was like an 8-ball jacket, but it had a suede football field on the back. This was big-time stuff back then!

Unfortunately, it started to get dark, and I had a pretty good distance to walk home. On the way home, I remember walking past a White Castle on Evergreen Street. I had started to go in and grab two or three burgers, but I exchanged a glance with a group of four or five older guys sitting at a window table. I will never forget the look that one of them gave me as he jumped up to pay the server and rushed to the door. Although there are some things that I learned the hard way, I wasn't going to let this become one of them. I ran as fast as I could, and I think I only stopped twice all the way home. I said very early that you can always change the venue that you are in and in this case I did just that. I didn't have to wait around and wonder if they were coming for my jacket or not. Technically, I guess it was my sister's jacket. Life was hard in Detroit growing up, but I learned so much about influence, leverage and negotiating life at a young age.

Luckily, I went from learning how to negotiate life growing up in Detroit to focusing on how to influence better leadership opportunities at Michigan State. Conservatively, my high school was at least 90 percent African American, maybe even 95 percent. In contrast, Michigan State University was at best 5 percent African American at the time. Talk about culture shock, right! I remember seeing Eastern Indians for the first time in front of the International Center Food Court next to the stadium and thinking, "I didn't know their skin could be darker than mine." For some of my classmates, the cultural adjustment was a bit too much and some of my friends from Detroit didn't make it all four years in East Lansing, MI.

On the other hand, I loved it! I studied more than just my books. I submerged myself in the people, the culture, the food, the languages, the upbringings, and the mindsets. In Detroit, I spent most of my time avoiding negative outcomes. For the first time in life, I felt like I could more so focus on driving positive outcomes. I have luckily felt this way ever since.

After graduating from Michigan State, my path has been an endless journey and quest for leadership. On that journey, I have only formally interviewed for one job. The rest of the opportunities were about who I knew and what motivated them to want to work with me. This only put me in a position to negotiate leadership roles and growth in my career. The rest of my leadership quest was up to me to leverage concepts in this book.

Lastly, along that leadership journey, I have received some amazing blessings. Many people have poured knowledge, trust, and belief into me. Now, I find myself sharing knowledge, trust, and belief every chance I get with colleagues, mentees, family, and friends. It wasn't until I went into private practice when I realized that I had to balance this love in my heart with being able to pay the bills. For a second, I honestly stopped being so accessible because I felt like I had to choose my livelihood over others. However, this didn't feel right. That is when I created the last and final rule for now.

Rule #12: When you find yourself giving away $2,500 of advice from the kindness of your heart, at least negotiate a $25 lunch for the hunger in your stomach.

At first, I felt bad for asking for value in return when leveraging Rule #12. This is until I realized the people who made sense to pour into, felt good about pouring back into me. Either way, usually when the bill comes, I often picked it up anyway. However, there is something special about the thought of those who you give energy, having no problems giving you energy right back.

All in all, I hope "The Dynamics of Leverage" has accelerated your journey to better. Whether your quest for leadership, your desire for quality of life, or again, your heart fulfillment of a good lunch conversation, thank you for the investment in yourself and good luck!

Bonus Content

12 Influence Rules for
Leadership, Life, & Lunch

Rule #1: If you aren't feeling your situation, feel free to change the vibe or the venue.

Rule #2: Always know the people you are dealing with and the things which motivate them to deal with you.

Rule #3: If all else fails, call out their process flaws to enhance your leverage.

Rule #4: Make sure your deals are "ROCK" solid to avoid buyer's remorse.

Rule #5: If you can't prove the value to yourself, it may be even harder proving it to someone else.

Rule #6: Almost everything in life is negotiable and other things are oftentimes worth confirming that they are not!

Rule #7: Most Negotiation Gatherers Proactively Game Plan well and most Negotiation Hunters have great Reactive Gameplay, but great influencers leaders understand, respect, and execute both!

Rule #8: Never allow anyone to decide when you are ready until you are truly ready.

Rule #9: Know Your MLOP like your ABC's.

Rule #10: The person who understands Leverage Philosophies can lead a discussion from time to time, however, the person who often applies Leverage Philosophies tend to control the relationship most of the time.

Rule #11: Not all of us negotiate and influence outcomes for a living, however, all of us should negotiate and influence outcomes for a better quality of life.

Rule #12: When you find yourself giving away $2,500 of advice from the kindness of your heart, at least negotiate a $25 lunch for the hunger in your stomach.

Special Thanks

Thanks to God for always showing me there is an audience when I feel unheard and there is light when I feel like I can't see the right path.

Thanks to my mother Clarissa and my father Floyd. There is something about your joint DNA that created me and the mixture of complexity and simplicity that makes me unique. Thanks for your lifelong development and love!

Thanks to my sisters Andrea, Meka, and Timika for taking that DNA and altering it just enough to allow me to relate to those women in the world who love my work and continuously invest in me professionally.

Thanks to my brother Aaron R. Smith for confirming that good guys really do finish first as we struggled together for better in the streets of Detriot.

Thanks to Tony Milikin, SVP & CPO at AB-InBev for believing an inner city kid could help him develop world-class procurement organizations. You are my Negotiation Hunter action figure.

Lastly, thank you Katrina, Marcela, and Ethel for asking me if I finished my book every time I got caught up with and in life. Hey ladies, it's finished!

Made in the USA
Columbia, SC
01 March 2021

33749788R00076